GARY H JAMES

Beyond The Closet

Cover Design: Ali Collins Illustration

Follow me on

Twitter: @GJ_EntFocus

Email me: GaryHJames@Virginmedia.com

DISCLAIMER

This is a work of creative non-fiction. Names and identifying features have been changed to protect the identity of certain parties. The author in no way represents any company, corporation, or brand, mentioned herein. The views expressed in this memoir are solely those of the author. Although based on true events, some scenarios and characters have been changed or invented to add a layer of interest for the reader.

First edition

ISBN: 9798693286955

This book was professionally typeset on Reedsy.
Find out more at reedsy.com

Contents

Introduction

I first started writing this book over 15 years ago when I was not that long in to my new life as a gay man. I was still scared and stubborn and didn't want to be seen as a stereotype.

I wanted to write a book based on my own experiences of coming out to explain the process to those who will never have to go through it. My hope was to educate, in particular, straight people as to what it is like to come out and what life as a gay man at the start of the new Millennium was all about.

What I didn't realise at the time was it was actually more a cathartic journey for me to come to terms with my sexuality and be happy in my own skin. Something which I am, more and more, although there are still occasions I find myself sneaking back in my shell.

I know that now, more than ever, gay rights have come a long way and I'm very grateful to have been born in the age and culture that I have been. I know that in other countries and religions, being gay is unacceptable, illegal or even a death sentence. That said, it's still much easier to be straight in my opinion because that's the norm and people are generally happier dealing with what they know and can easily label.

My story begins at the end of 1999 and already in just 20 short years, gay rights and society has moved on so much that many of the stories in my book may not connect with someone who is 20 years old and coming out today.

It's perhaps for this reason that this book was left semi-completed for years, but now I feel the need to return to it, finish it and get it out there. If one person can find something they relate to and not feel so alone then I've done a good job.

The story I'm about to tell you is an open and honest account of how I felt about coming out and my life as a gay man. Although based on true events, I have applied creative license changing scenarios and characters for entertainment purposes and also to protect the innocent and the not so innocent!

For some the scene is part of being gay and for others they feel the scene represents a stereotype. What I have learned is that neither of those views is wrong, it's completely down to the individual. The more representation gay people have in society in all their guises, the more the stereotype of a gay man will evolve.

Whether you're gay, straight, bi or anywhere else on the spectrum of sexuality, I hope you find my story interesting, funny and sad in equal measure, because that's how I feel having lived it.

Chapter 1

"Come on, tell us. Who in the office would you shag?" Jane asked Will. He was being his usual shy self when it came to such matters.

"Only needs to be your Top 3, and in no particular order," I added. It's a simple question that I'm sure many of us have asked or been asked on numerous occasions (especially those involving work mates and alcohol) and yet the answer to this innocuous request would change my life forever.

A group from work had gone bowling and after I'd whupped all their asses with a sublime multiple-strike game, only three of us were left having a cheeky half in the bar; Jane, Will and I. As music from the likes of Christina Aguilera, Five and Eiffel 65 gentle mingled with the tumbling of skittles and the occasional whoop of excitement, our mood was very much upbeat after a fun night. Now, though, with that one question the atmosphere had suddenly turned tense.

After much avoiding of our gazes and lots of 'Oooh,ummms,' Will was struggling to answer. Jane and I were beginning to get very bored of waiting for his answer when he finally crumbled and said,

"I don't want to shag any of the girls in the office." Before either of us had finished tutting and rolling our eyes, ready to push him further, Will muttered, "Because I'm gay."

It was one of those situations where someone drops a bombshell and you can feel the shock visualizing on your face; mouth gaping, eyes bulging and eyebrows rising. I fought hard to hide that face, as I reeled a little from his revelation. My subconscious, sensible side, pulled me back to the moment at hand and told me I needed to not make this a big thing.

"The question still remains: who in the office would you shag?" I said, before adding, "Present company is a given, of course, so needs to be excluded." Clearly, I didn't need a dent to my ego or an awkward confession of love from Will. Jane hadn't quite managed to hide the shock on her face but gladly played along. Will beamed in front of us, tension washing away and he soon began to revel in the opportunity to share his male office crushes. The relief was oozing out of him, quickly followed by the excitement of finally being able to confess how he'd always quite fancied this one and that one in the office. Jane and I mocked him for his poor taste.

The conversation took a step toward the serious as our shock was replaced with a thousand questions: *When did you know? How do you know? Who else knows?*

"Well apart from a rather failed attempt at telling my mum that I thought I was gay about four years ago and a telling a girl whilst I was at Uni, this is me just starting to tell people." Will said.

"I think deep down I'd known I was different from being a little boy and definitely as a teenager but I just buried those feelings and lead what I thought of as 'normal' life." Will paused before continuing,

"I guess I really didn't want to be gay growing up and I kept telling myself that I just hadn't met the right girl." Jane and I were respectfully silent for once as we listened eagerly.

"I know it sounds clichéd but that is truly how I convinced myself I wasn't gay and now well I think I'm sick of trying to hide who I am."

What Will had said made me realise that society definitely pushes a very certain way of life and unless you revel in being different, we all try to conform to the same model; boy meets girl, they get married, have children and live happily ever after.

"So, have you never had a girlfriend?" asked Jane. Will let out a nervous laugh and shook his head.

"There was one girl. She was actually one of my neighbours growing up, so we'd known each other for years." Will took a big gulp of his beer before going on.

"I think I knew that she liked me and she was a nice girl. I thought maybe she could be the one. Maybe if I slept with her it would unlock my straight desires and everything would be fine." Will looked thoughtful as his gaze fell to the floor and his shoulders slumped a little.

"About three years ago I went to see her at Uni and we went for a pizza and everything was going fine. When we got home I went to kiss her and she kissed me back, but..well...nothing happened down below. I knew then that I was kidding myself and I told her that I thought I was gay."

I hadn't realised how intently I was leaning in to listen to the story and let out an involuntary gasp. Will's eyes seem to linger on mine for a split second before he went on.

"Poor Sophie. I should never have given her false hope. It made for an awkward weekend I'll tell you that."

Will explained that, like we had just done, Sophie asked the usual question; *'If you've never been with a man or a woman, how would you know you were gay?'* He told her that he just knew and that he was definitely gay. It's strange how the first question many straight people ask gay people is *'How do you know?'* or seem to think they can cure them, like it's an ailment: *Take two women daily with a bottle of wine before and after dinner and if your gayness hasn't cleared up in two weeks, come back and we'll up the dose.*

As the clock ticked by, we agreed it was time to draw the night to a close and we laughed and joked as we reassured Will and headed out to the car park. As I shut my car door, my head was spinning. Adrenaline was surging through me. Will was gay. Many thoughts raced through my mind. I was dealing with empathy for Will and a feeling that I needed to reassure him, but why was I also excited? Truth was that for many years I'd suppressed the possibility that I might be bi-sexual or gay.

On the drive home, I rode out waves of fear - what if I was gay? Would Will already know this? – and excitement at maybe not feeling like I was the only one who had these feelings; that I wasn't the only 'abnormal' one out there. If nothing else, I hoped that Will could be trusted to be the ear I suddenly so desperately needed. Surely he could help me equate my feelings against those of his own and help me decipher if I was gay or not. Maybe it was just a moderate interest in the same sex in a similar way that I liked the look of rubber, but couldn't imagine ever being dressed head-to-toe complete with a cue ball in my mouth? Will wouldn't judge me, would he? The cage that housed these darkest thoughts was suddenly unlocked, yet somehow the voice of fear seemed quieter in my head.

As I drove home, it occurred to me that I'd seen something the other day that I thought was odd, but now made complete sense. A few nights earlier a group from work had been out clubbing and several people had stayed over at my flat. Next morning, Will came in to my bedroom with a cup of tea and I caught his glance dart towards my sleeping shorts, which were unfortunately riding that little bit too high; an odd thing for a straight guy to do, but not for a gay guy. As I walked into my flat I couldn't help but chuckle at that thought – Gotcha!

Even though it was late, I wanted to call Will to confirm everything I'd said in the bar; that it didn't change anything between us and that I was there for him. I also wanted to blurt out how relieved I was that I might not be the only one, how I needed to explain my thoughts and feelings to him and that he had to tell me if I was gay or not. Then I realised how incredibly selfish I was being. This was about Will, not me and he must be feeling a strange mix of emotions after coming out to Jane and I.

I picked up the phone and felt my throat dry up as I dialled his number. I coughed out a nervous giggle.

"Hi Will. Long time no speak" I said.

"Er Hi Gary. What's up?" he replied and I could hear the apprehension in his voice.

"I just wanted to reassure you that we're still friends and nothing you've said tonight changes that." I said.

"Phew. Was worried for a minute you were calling to tell me the opposite." Said Will.

"Come on. Do you really think a guy who likes pop music is going to have an issue with someone who's gay? I'd never be able to go to a Kylie concert ever again if that was the case." I joked.

We chatted for about thirty minutes and I just couldn't help myself; I was flirting with him. I'm a very flirtatious person so that's nothing new, but this time I was playing with fire. I even jokingly offered myself as a willing victim if he needed to practice his blow job technique. I didn't reveal any of the way I was feeling on this call, but did offer my ear should he ever need to talk.

I put the phone down that night with an admiration for Will and the courage he had to accept he was gay and to be able to tell his friends. At the age of 25, Will had never enjoyed being with someone and I don't just mean the sexual side of things. He'd never had a partner to slob on the sofa with, go on holiday with, to care for and be cared for back. That's the sad thing; Will is such a lovely guy and had he been straight there's no way that he would've been single. In fact, he was considered one of the most eligible bachelors in the office by many of the girls. If only they knew!

Soon my thoughts moved away from Will and as I lay in my bed longing for sleep to take me, I went round in circles – you're gay, you're not gay, you're gay. It soon turned into a different question 'What are you going to do if you are gay?' which then spun out into hundreds of related questions – What will Mum and Dad say? What about my brothers and sister? How will I tell them? How will I get a boyfriend? Do I have to tell the people at work? and so the night went on. It's safe to say I didn't get much sleep that night and it left me with the one conclusion: I needed to talk through my feelings with Will.

Chapter 2

Next morning, as I wiped the sleepy dust from my eyes, last night's events instantly replayed in my mind as if someone had pressed play.

Will was gay and I thought that I might be too. Nah, that was ridiculous, I was just quite open minded and enjoyed various sexual fantasies. The thoughts I had about men were just that – fantasies. Fantasies that I would probably never even act out, after all I knew that some of my other fantasies just didn't play out in the same way as they did in your mind; never again was I going to wear handcuffs.

As I showered and got dressed in a rush for work, I couldn't change the channel; it was The Gary Gayathon Live Debate going on in my head. That caged beast that I unleashed last night was now fighting back against my sensible and incredibly scared, side. Maybe I could go to lunch with Will and get it all out of my head. Then again, maybe he wouldn't be a neutral judge after all, maybe he'd persuade me I was gay so that he wouldn't have to go through coming out on his own?

Maybe Jane would be better; she was great with Will last night - why should she be any different to me? We had grown quite close of late.

NO! screamed the fear in my head,

Don't tell anyone just leave it for a few days and give yourself time to think. You're probably just confused, it's not been long since you split from Ruth and you're just lost and lonely, so every option seems good right now.

Maybe my fear was right. I had only been single for about three months since the breakup with my girlfriend of over seven years, and as much as I didn't like to admit it, I was still in a very vulnerable state. I'd take my own advice and suppress my gay feelings for the time being. Maybe I should stay out of Will's way for a few days too.

Oh no, there he is chatting to Jane and I'm going have to walk straight past them both to get to my desk.

"Morning!" I said, as chirpily as I could muster. I know I was being paranoid but as I walked away from them I heard them laugh and felt ashamed and angry at the thought of Will telling Jane about our late night phone conversation.

As I turned on my computer and gave the customary nods to the rest of the team, I let sense take over and calmed myself. I knew that Will wouldn't be telling Jane about our call and even if he was, she wouldn't think it anything more than me being my cheeky self. I forced myself to focus on my work and took to doing the marketing plan that I'd be avoiding like the plague for the last month. I needed to get my brain into something that would take up my full consciousness and stop me going over everything again.

I kept my head down and got through the day, and as I made my dinner that evening, I actually felt quite smug that I'd managed to knock out a stellar marketing plan. My mind had calmed down and I was now laughing at how wound up and confused I'd been. I wasn't gay. Sure, I liked pop music and was in touch with my feminine side, but that was all it was.

I couldn't believe how silly I was being, just trying to jump on the bandwagon, keep up with the Wills, so to speak.

I was exhausted, yet in a weird relaxed state as I numbed my mind further by watching Eastenders. The phone went and I answered expecting it to be my mother telling me all about the latest going-ons back home and was surprised to hear Will on the line.

"Hi Gary, it's Will," he said tentatively. "Oh, Hi Will, how are you?" I replied with some hesitation.

"Yeah, good thanks. Was just ringing to see how you're doing. You seemed a bit distant at work today and …well…I thought maybe you were avoiding me because of ..well..what I told you and Jane last night" I felt the panic surging through me; he was on to me. I had totally avoided him, not because of the reason he thinks, but because of my own worries. I couldn't have him thinking that it was anything to do with him and his revelation. This was a very delicate time for him too.

"Gary?" he prompted.

"Sorry, I was distracted by the TV. Peggy just gave Kathy a good telling off." I let out a laugh and hoped he would too. It bought me time to compose myself and so I continued,

"Don't be stupid. I told you last night that I'm a willing victim so why would I be avoiding you? In fact, I thought we were supposed to meet in the toilets, Cubicle 2 at 12.30 for your first attempt?"

What was I doing? Flirting again, digging myself in deeper. I quickly took the conversation back to the more serious.

"I had to do that bloody marketing plan that you sales guys have been hassling me for, and in truth I'd been putting it off for weeks, so needed to get my head down today."

"Yeah I saw it. Looks great. So we're all cool, yeah?" He still sounded a bit worried.

"Well I am, don't know about you, I thought that shirt you had on last night went out in the 80s" I said. We both relaxed into the conversation and it soon became the usual light-hearted banter about work colleagues.

By the end of the conversation I was feeling curious again, so asked Will how he felt now he'd come out to myself and Jane and we got talking about him being gay again. This was my way of fishing for information to reconcile against my own gay feelings.

"I have known deep down since I was a child" said Will.

"I remember playing with friends and I'd always want to be with the boys. I guess most boys do so it wasn't unusual, but I knew that there was something I felt when I saw Jonny Maycroft take his top off when we played doctors that made me feel close to him."

I listened intently, giving him the space to tell his story, whilst I secretly compared my life to his.

"In my teens, I got more and more possessive of my best friend and to all intents and purposes I think I saw us as couple, but without anything sexual going on." Will continued.

"I remember trying to talk him out of going out with girls, always putting them down, but of course his hormones were raging and he didn't listen to me." He chuckled as he realised how annoying he must've been to the girls that were after his mate.

I decided to probe deeper and asked,

"So you've never fancied a girl?"

"Not really," he said.

"And you've never done more than kiss a girl?" I probed.

"Nope. I tried that one time but it just wasn't happening."

He laughed coyly.

"Anyway, I'd best leave you to it," he paused slightly,

"..And thanks for listening. I really appreciate it. You're a good friend"

I was racked with guilt as little did he know that he was actually helping me enormously too.

"Ah don't be daft. What are friends for?" I said.

"Actually, friends are for drinking with aren't they? So how about we see who's around to hit the town on Saturday?"

As Will agreed to a night out and we said our goodbyes, I was left feeling relieved. Will had never fancied girls, yet I'd had lots of girlfriends and a fairly active sex life with my ex right up until we split. Will had always known he was gay too, yet my gay thoughts only crept in when I was in my late teens. It was another point to Team Hetero!

Chapter 3

Saturday night arrived and I'd managed to get a group of five to go out drinking before heading to Stages nightclub. Keeping it cheap and cheerful, we went to the local Irish bar, Scruffy Murphys and knocked back several drinks to get our dancing courage up for the club.

Everyone was in good spirits, especially Jane and I who had been winding Will up as one of his top three office shags, David, was out that night. He was mock grinding against Will in his best JLo' booty-shaking impression and Will was looking incredibly uncomfortable. He tried to push David away, much to the amusement of Jane and I who decided to take up where David had left off, taking a leg each to bump and grind with. This time Will loosened up and joined in.

At the end of the night we all piled out of the club and put Jane in one cab and David and Michelle in another. As usual, Will was staying at mine so we made the short walk back to my flat. I started to feel incredibly nervous and giggly. Maybe it was the drink or maybe it was that bootylicious dance but I didn't really know what to say. I think Will was feeling the same as he went very quiet too, but still had a smirk on his face. I broke the silence,

"Did you see that guy who was trying to pull Jane tonight?

Oh my God, what a Behemoth!" Will replied,

"Yeah, I didn't fancy hers much." We both laughed a little too much as we reached the gates to my flat. As I pulled the gate open I gestured for him to go first and he indicated for me to go first instead and this carried on Chuckle Brothers style - to me, to you, to me, to you – until we both moved forward and our hands brushed against each other making us recoil shyly. Embarrassed, I rushed through the gate and didn't stop until I got to my front door. It had felt good to touch his hand; the tingly feeling that shot up my arm as our skin touched. What was going to happen now? We were just friends, right, and I wasn't gay was I? But then again I was single, and maybe I should put my gayness to the ultimate test?

"I'll stick the kettle on. What you having?" I shouted from the kitchen as I took off my jacket and flung it on the chair. Will shouted back, "Tea" as he headed into the toilet.

I suddenly felt very nervous and excited again and quickly whizzed round tidying things away. Will came in and sat next to me on the sofa and I handed him his tea. We sat in silence, both sipping our tea and looking at various things in the room, trying to make small talk.

"I like your American Beauty poster. Have you seen the film?" asked Will.

"Yes. Yes I have." I replied.

"Me too." said Will.

"Oh god, what a ridiculous headline on Heat magazine - Ally McBeal is responsible for unisex toilets coming to the UK apparently." he continued.

"Really? I didn't even know we had unisex toilets." I said. What I'd been dying to ask Will on the way home from the club was how he felt about David's dancing. I decided now was as good a time as any.

"So, did you love it when David was grinding against your leg?" I asked.

"No! Well, not really….maybe a little," he replied as we both laughed more naturally this time.

"I've always thought he was a bit on the gay side actually. He's very close to his male housemates. Maybe that's just laddishness but I find it a bit odd. You pick anything up with your gay sonar?" I asked.

"I believe it's called gaydar. What sort of fag hag do you think you're going to be if you go around calling it gay sonar?" Will replied. I gave him a playful punch.

"I wish David was gay," he continued and he paused slightly, his mind wandering off into some fantasy no doubt.

"But I think he's just a lad. Besides isn't he shagging half of the secretaries in the office?"

"Yeah, you're probably right. Well what about the office, anyone else make your gaydar bleep?" I said using my fingers to air speech mark the word gaydar.

Will rubbed his chin panto style.

"Hmmm, well Ben in Customer Services is a bit suspect and Don is camp as Christmas, but strangely I think he's actually straight. Then there's Hugo in accounts. All the munters." He went to say something else and then stopped and laughed.

"What?" I said "Tell me!" He looked really sheepish as he said,

"I actually thought you might be gay when I first met you." He let that linger for a moment,

"But obviously then I met your girlfriend and got to know you, and realised you weren't – although you do fit the munter profile." He laughed to try and take the sting out of his comment.

At first I was stunned. What made him think I was gay? Did I give out gay signals or something? Rather than be angry with him, I said,

"Well I'm not gay but I have experimented whilst I was at school." After I'd said that, my fear was ringing in my ears: *why did you say that?*

"Really? What happened?" Will asked excitedly.

I decided to quickly change the subject.

"Another time, I'm knackered. Can you be trusted to share my double bed and not try and touch me?" I joked.

He looked disappointed but said,

"I'll try my best. You can tie my hands behind my back if you like."

"It's not your hands I'm worried about" I joked. "Go on, you can use the bathroom first while I wash up these cups."

Plenty of people had shared my double bed since Ruth moved out, both men and women but it had only ever been as friends and a more comfy place for them to sleep. Will had previously too and I'd thought nothing of it, but this was the first time since he'd come out. I stood in the kitchen gormlessly washing out the same mug over and over as I tried to decide what my next move would be. As much as the fear was there, it was also making me feel incredibly excited. I felt my rebellious streak coming to the fore; *no one has to know, it could be good experience for you both.*

"Bathroom's free," said Will, popping his head around the door, making me jump.

"Oh right, will be right there."

I stared at myself long and hard in the bathroom mirror. This could be it Gary, the moment you never allowed yourself to believe you wanted. It could prove to you that you are actually straight if you start something and there's no passion or interest. You don't have to do anything. He might not even be interested. Just because he's gay, doesn't mean he fancies you or is going to try it on with you. I brushed my teeth, took a deep breath and gave myself a final encouraging smile and muttered *'que sera sera....whatever will be will be'*

Will was lying on his side in the foetal position facing away from me. I slid gently under the duvet and lay on my back, suddenly wide awake.

"Night," said Will.

"It was with a friend the night before my 18th birthday." I began my story. Will didn't move but I could tell he was listening intently.

"He'd always been quite arty and adventurous you see." I waited briefly for acknowledgement from Will, but nothing came so I continued my confessional.

"It was the night before my eighteenth birthday and we were sleeping in the sitting room as relatives had my bedroom. He was on the sofa, and I was on a mattress on the floor." I didn't really care if Will was asleep or awake; this story was now more of an acknowledgement to myself.

"We were chatting away as you do, and then my friend, Ed, starts telling me about this girl at college that he'd love to get it on with. He started describing in detail what he'd like to do. I could tell he was getting turned on and I was too. I jokingly said *'Give me a blow job would you?'* He told me to go suck myself. *'Would if I could, but I can't reach'* I told him. There was a slight pause and then he said *'Do you really want me to?'* Thinking that this was never going to happen, I pushed on. What I didn't realise was that my goading was like a red rag to a bull with Ed: Tell him he can't do something and he wants to do it even more. I was so nervous and tingled all over as he moved from the sofa to my mattress. Both of us were giggling like Japanese school girls as he said *'Get it out then'*. I didn't know what to do, but he made the decision for me by pulling my shorts down and revealing my erection. It was all very clumsy, but I was buzzing. My body was shivering despite being the middle of summer. He gave me a blow job and then I returned the favour. We justified it as pals helping each other out with a task that we'd have done ourselves were we physically capable. It was very mechanical – no kissing or anything, just straight to it."

As I finished my story I turned to Will.

"Will? You awake?" I touched his arm and could feel him shaking in what I recognised as the same shivers that I'd had as my friend came down to the mattress. I felt myself go instantly hard, rolled him over on to his back and kissed him slowly and softly. He responded by pulling me closer….this was going to be far from mechanical.

Chapter 4

I lay awake in bed listening to the tell-tale heavy breathing that meant Will had nodded off. What had I done? It wasn't that it hadn't been exciting and I had certainly enjoyed it, but what did that mean for me now? Was I bi-sexual? I was suddenly hit with a wave of guilt over my ex-girlfirend Ruth. Despite the fact that we'd split up about three months ago, I couldn't help but feel I'd just betrayed her. Maybe it was more a knowing in me that this can't have happened overnight; a realisation that I'd been carrying these feelings for a long time.

I felt a panic welling up inside me and quickly, but gently, slid out of the bed so as not to wake Will. I headed to the bathroom and splashed water on my face, before taking a few good long deep breaths. I looked at myself in the mirror and my eyes were blurry with tears. The fear was overwhelming. I gave myself a whispered talking to and headed into the kitchen to make myself a cup of tea.

As I walked over to the sofa, I noticed an old photo album on the shelf and picked it up. It was mostly from a holiday Ruth and I had been on in Gran Canaria the previous summer. We looked every bit the happy couple and I thought we were, but now I wasn't so sure.

* * *

Ruth was a very shy character and that made her all the more attractive to me in the beginning. There was something about the quiet ones I liked; a trait I blame on my mother who was always inviting waifs and strays, be they human or animal, into our house as I grew up. Not that Ruth was a mongrel - far from it. She was quite the English rose with her pale skin, black hair and pouting red lips. She was seventeen when we met and had just moved to the sleepy little Hampshire village that I'd called home since my dad had retired out of the army four years prior. I was instantly attracted to her and it wasn't long until we were officially an item and finishing our A Levels together.

The first cracks in our relationship began to show when we finished school. We both decided to go to the same university, but after just two weeks, she decided that it wasn't for her and she went home. I was having a whale of a time, loving living in a shared house and being able to go out clubbing and fend for myself for the first time. She was stuck at her folk's house and got her first job in an office. I remember her suggesting that we should split up or take a break when I was at university, but I was adamant that we shouldn't – our love would conquer all! Besides, it felt like she was only saying it for my benefit and didn't really want to split up, she just felt it was the right thing to do.

Thinking back on my time at university now, she did hamper my experience slightly by coming to visit most weekends. I often felt I was missing out on hanging out with my new friends and the fun things they seemed to be getting up to. Following university, I landed a job at a reputable car manufacturing company on the outskirts of London and Ruth agreed to move with me to the area. She managed to get herself an admin job at another local company and we rented our first flat together. The initial excitement of buying furniture and playing at grown-ups had begun to fade as the months went on. Yet again I found myself wanting to hang out with my new work friends and felt Ruth was becoming a ball and chain.

In recent months I knew that I wanted to split with her but I was too much of a coward. I also felt this huge guilt that I was her life, and to dump her would leave her with nothing and maybe she'd do something stupid.

She still hadn't made many friends: in contrast I loved going out and always felt that I was burdened by having to babysit her whenever she was persuaded to come out for the night. I'd tried my best to encourage her and bring her out of her shell in the years we spent together and despite things not always being great, I didn't want to give up on her. I was determined to make her more sociable and introduced her to my friends in the hope she'd see what fun she was missing out on. It was to little avail.

As time went on with Ruth, and the more I got out of the small Hampshire town mentality where I'd grown up, the more I noticed I was checking out guys. It may sound like weird logic, but when I was with Ruth, I used to tell myself that I eyed up lads rather than girls because then I wasn't cheating on her. Nothing was ever going to happen with them, it was my own inbuilt cheat-safe mechanism or something. If it had been looking at ladies in that way, then that would be like cheating on Ruth.

I suppressed those slightly abnormal feelings and got on with having a girlfriend and tried to be like most other couples. In fact, it was Ruth who started the ball rolling for us to split. If she hadn't, maybe I'd be one of those men who is married with children and really not happy.

We both knew that things had gotten really stale between us and I think we had grown up and apart from each other. What exactly happened to make Ruth break up with me I don't entirely know.

Ruth was acting a bit strange when I got home from work one day. Almost excitedly, she said she wanted to try living just as friends to inject some fun back into the relationship. I was stunned as I never expected her to instigate a split and to this day I'm not sure if the real reason wasn't that she fancied a guy from work. We only had a one bedroom flat with a double bed and the thought of sharing a bed with your lover but trying to just be friends to me was all wrong. The funny thing is that after talking she had nothing to say so I went to my best friend Amanda's house and cried on her shoulder. When I came back home, ironically Ruth told me that if I hadn't run away that night, the relationship may have been saved through talking about it.

* * *

Back in the post-gay-experience light of well past midnight early December 1999, I sat on the sofa looking at our faces smiling up from the poolside bar photo. Ruth wasn't a bad person in any way, she just wasn't right for me and our relationship had long outstayed its welcome. Now just a few short months on from the heartbreak and sorting who got the posh cutlery, here I was with a sated man in my bed. I felt the blood drain from my face at the thought of her finding out.

She wouldn't believe that this was a new thing and might even think she'd somehow turned me gay.

There was that gay word again. Surely I was bi-sexual? I shut the photo album and pulled a nearby blanket around myself as I curled into a ball. My brain was beyond frazzled and I needed to try and get some sleep. I put the TV on with the volume turned low and found a repeat of a recent Who Wants To Be A Millionaire. I didn't care what it was, I just needed something to distract me from myself until sleep decided to take me.

Chapter 5

Next morning and I'd hardly slept a wink all night after drifting off on the sofa. As I rubbed my cricked neck, I was more confused than ever.

I'd gone and done it. I'd had my first proper gay encounter. On the plus side, I was single and wasn't hurting anyone. It was just a bit of fun and I'm sure next time I'd go out it'd be a girl I'd take home. Hell, I was just doubling my options, right? When you broke it down, did it actually matter that I'd played with a penis rather than a vagina? I stifled a laugh at how ridiculous sex is.

I sat at the table staring out the window for what felt like hours holding, what by now was, a cold cup of tea trying to make myself feel better. It wasn't working.

"Morning!" said Will rather chirpily. He was definitely looking like the cat who had gotten the cream. He'd had his first gay experience and of course he was feeling good; he knew he was gay.

It was making me feel sick to look at him and know what I'd done. Actually, the truth was that I was sick with fear at what it meant for my life now. How could I be gay? I'd not long split up with my girlfriend of over seven years. It was just temporary insanity. I was just desperate to feel loved and was rebelling, wasn't I?

It dawned on me that I'd actually spent most of my life defending myself from those who accused me of being gay. Could that be why it'd taken me so long to realise that I might actually be gay or bi-sexual? Was I just trying to conform with society? Was I being stubborn to all the people who thought they could see the gay in me before I could?

"You alright Gary?" Will interrupted my thoughts. "You look a bit out of it". I just wanted him to leave, I couldn't deal with him being near me and forcing me to accept what I'd done.

"Yeah, just shouldn't have had those cocktails. I feel soooo hungover and have barely slept." I couldn't look him in the eye but could tell he wasn't buying my story. "I'm going to go back to bed. Help yourself to breakfast." I managed a weak smile as I walked past him.

Next time I saw him was about thirty minutes later when he came hopefully into the bedroom and whispered "Are you awake?" Of course I was but I pretended not to be. I felt the softness of his lips as he nervously kissed my cheek and whispered, "I'll call you later."

Oh God, what had I done? Here was this lovely guy who had just come out, I'd led him on and now I was giving him the cold shoulder. He didn't deserve to be treated like this, but right now I'd have to worry about myself. I'd have to call him later and explain, but for now I had some soul searching to do. It was time for a nice hot bath and a deep dip in Lake Me. Could I really be turning gay at the age of twenty three?

I needed to play detective on my own life, look back through my memories for clues as to whether I really was gay and had always been so or whether it was just a phase brought on by the failure of my relationship with Ruth.

Truth is, I hate failing at anything – scares the shit out of me. I'm not sure where this has come from, perhaps partly from my mother. She's always doted on me and my siblings, but I have always had a special relationship with her. She's my rock and I hers. She has always encouraged me and told me I can achieve anything I set out to do. So far I was doing well. I had good qualifications and a degree, passed my driving test first time and got a good job straight out of university. I was a Marketing Executive for a car manufacturer and although I had no interest in the product it was a good, sensible job. It didn't matter that my heart had always longed for a job in TV; that was unrealistic and I should use my sensible Business Studies degree to make a good wage for myself and progress up the ladder to support my future family. I had the pretty girlfriend to give me that family too, until three months ago.

Failing at anything is catastrophic for me and I'd also feel like I was letting my mum down as well as myself. Insight No.2 into my psyche is that I really worry what other people think and hate being judged, and so I live in fear of trying certain things in case I fail and then have to face up to people thinking I'm a failure. This of course I know is a complete waste of my time as most people don't care and those who do will be nothing but supportive of me. It's also very hypocritical of me as I can be very judgmental of others.

From a young age I had shown signs of being gay or more feminine, often enduring many a 'poof' comment. In fact, thinking back on it now I was probably bullied to an extent. I've not been scarred by this or at least I don't think I have. In fact, I think it made me rebel against being gay. Was that what had happened? Had I built a self-defence mechanism that protected me from the bullies? If I had let myself be gay then wouldn't the bullying have gotten worse from them and from my brothers too? Is the mind clever enough to blot things out like that, almost as a self-preservation tool?

Now I was grown up and had moved away from the bullies and my family and was free of Ruth too. Had this freed my mind to let my true feelings come to the fore? Was it Will that was the catalyst?

I don't know how long I'd been lying in the bath but I was starting to get prune fingers. I was startled when I heard the key turn in the front door.

"Gary? Are you in?" Came Ruth's familiar voice.

"I'm in the bath," I shouted back, puzzled as to why she was back in the flat and feeling a bit put out that she just walked straight back in to what I now considered my flat. Technically, we were both still on the lease until it finished at the end of January, but she'd found a work mate with a spare room and moved out. I couldn't believe it when she came into the bathroom and sat on the toilet. I manoeuvred the little bath foam that was left to cover my modesty.

"What do you think you're doing, Ruth?" I said. Ruth just laughed, looking straight at my quickly eroding foam fig leaf.

"Come on Gary, I've seen it all before. More than seen it actually." She gave a coquettish smile, before slumping into a downtrodden look as if remembering that she wasn't supposed to be happy.

I was scrunching up trying to keep my dignity, unhappy at her intrusion.

"What do you want, Ruth?" I asked sharply. She gave one of her trade mark sighs; I knew she was attention hungry.

"Things aren't going great over at my new place." She said. What did she want me to do about it?

"Sorry to hear that. You just need to give it time." I said "Do you mind if we carry this on once I've gotten out and dressed?"

She gave another involuntary smirk "Sure. I'll go put the kettle on" she said and left the room. As I got up to get out of the bath she popped her head back in again.

"Everything still where it used to be?" she asked as innocently as she could.

"YES!" I shouted angrily. She had clearly popped in for a good look.

She mumbled as she left the room,

"Yep, looks like it's all still where I left it." She turned with a big grin on her face. I locked the door loudly to make a point and then proceeded to dry myself, wrapping the towel around my waist and heading to the bedroom where I speedily pulled on some pants and jeans. As I turned around to look for my t-shirt, I nearly jumped out of my skin to see Ruth stood looking at me. She was being quite coy and flicking her hair with a cheeky smile on her face as she started to walk towards me. I was frozen to the spot as she put her arms around me and whispered in my ear,

"I miss you." In that moment I felt utter contempt for her. She'd been the one who was super independent since we'd split and now she was in what was our bedroom telling me she missed me. I went to push her away and establish some space between us, but she was locked on as she tried to kiss me.

"What the hell do you think you're doing?" I shouted as we jostled.

"Come on, for old time's sake," she said, literally trying to trip me onto the bed. I leapt to my senses and pushed her away.

"No, Ruth! It's over, we're over," I said sternly, and she started to cry. My instinct was to hold her and tell her it would

27

be alright, but I was so angry at her trying to mess with my emotions that I went through to the kitchen.

"I'm going to get the tea. There are tissues on the side." I said curtly. Moments later, I heard the front door slam and she was gone.

I sat down more confused than I'd ever been. My ex-girlfriend who I thought I would marry, had forced a split between us and then acted like it was no big deal. I'd slept with Will last night and next day she'd come along practically begging me for sex and perhaps some kind of reconciliation. I laughed into my tea with disbelief at what was happening; these were crazy times.

Chapter 6

I started to imagine a parallel universe where being gay was equal in society to being straight, and wondered if I'd had the option of being gay growing up whether I'd have taken it. The thing is that I didn't know any gay people growing up. There were a couple of guys at school who took a pasting in sixth form for being camp but they were never out at school and had girlfriends galore. Even at university I didn't know any gay people although there were some guys who fit the stereotype, but it still wasn't prevalent.

I have always been intrigued by gay things though, slyly reading the odd gay magazine article or news piece. It seemed that many gay guys that I'd read about knew they were gay as they came down the birth canal and tried to pick out some nice wallpaper. I can't honestly remember thinking anything sexual until I was nine and had my first 'James Bond' kiss (i.e. open mouthed).

From then on I was a horny little guy and had girlfriends on and off, with the first longer term one when I was about 13. Well it lasted three months which at that age is long term. I didn't have anything but pervy thoughts on my mind. I loved snogging and groping and trying to move things to the next level although I didn't lose my virginity until I was with Ruth.

I suddenly remembered a time when I was about 12 years old. I was camping in my parent's back garden with a friend called John. John was the first guy at our school to hit puberty and I'd been strangely fascinated by him in the changing rooms after PE, sneaking glances without being caught. In the tent, we were messing around and play fighting, as boys do, when suddenly he pinned me on my back, opened my legs, placed a pillow there and pretended to shag me. I remember at the time it all being quite a laugh, but secretly being quite turned on by it too, although at that age I wasn't quite sure what that feeling was.

I needed to stop my brain from whirring round in overtime picking through old memories trying to decide if I was gay or not. I didn't want to be gay. That would mean being different, having to be what I'd been brought up to see as defective or inferior. How would I tell my brothers and my dad. I didn't even know how my mum and sister would take it, let alone all my friends?

I felt sick. I don't know whether it genuinely was the cocktails from the night before this time, or just the sheer panic, but the room was spinning and I had to rush to the toilet.

As I sat there on the bathroom floor, sick splattered chin and washed out skin, the tears came like a flood down my face. What had I done and what was I going to do now? I felt so alone in that moment. I had no one I could turn to. I daren't mention to any of my family or friends that I thought I might be gay. That would be too much like making it real; once you've said it out loud there's no going back. My eyes were red raw and I was so tired. I took my sobbing to the bedroom.

It wasn't a comfortable sleep, the dreams were coming in

30

a big jumbled heap. Waving Ruth goodbye as she went on a train journey; Running naked on a beach with Will, with all my friends and family angrily chasing behind us with meat cleavers – clearly my brain's way of expressing the fear.

As I awoke, a kind of calm descended over me. I was mentally and physically exhausted and couldn't seem to care about anything. My emotions were gone and now every thought was logical and black and white as my mind moved through a multitude of memories.

As I'd told Will last night, Ed was my only other sexual encounter with the same sex. I remembered vividly how after the deed had been done, neither Ed nor I knew what to say. We just said goodnight and I lay down to sleep with the consequences of what we'd done racing through my mind. Firstly, I'd cheated on Ruth, whether I could rationalise it away or not, and secondly I'd just sucked my first penis. It wasn't like we'd kissed or there had been a passionate build up, it was *'Here's my erection, pop that in your mouth please. Cheers Mate.'*

The following day we acted normally and avoided talking about it until later that night. We finally discussed what we'd done and convinced ourselves there was nothing gay about it; it just made practical sense. Before long though, we were at it again; we'd talked ourselves into it being ok.

We were very close as friends and I do think that sometimes you can confuse this for love. Looking back it really was just experimentation and being horny teens, we never tried to kiss each other nor hug. In some respects he really could've been anyone. I don't know how I managed to bury that as unimportant and experimenting. I know that it was really tough to see Ruth again afterwards knowing I'd cheated on her – something I never ever thought I could do – but was it proper cheating? At the time I had decided not, to ease my guilt no doubt. Poor Ruth, first she might have to deal with the fact her recent ex-boyfriend might be gay and secondly, I'd cheated on her with a man many years back, no matter how mechanical it was.

As I lay in bed, staring at the ceiling, I started to convince myself that I'd been gay all along. First, the memory of John in the tent and obviously worst of all, what had happened with Ed. I felt ashamed of myself for the last one; still can't believe I did that to Ruth.

I suddenly had a flashback to my first week at university. I remembered right at the start of my course being in a big hall full of stalls where people were trying to encourage you to sign up to the various societies. As I scanned the list I saw that there was a Gay & Lesbian society stall and decided that I'd stalk all the stalls around it to see what it was all about. Now, I'm sure sailing knots are really interesting, but for a landlover who'd be sick on a pedalo, I was not really listening as Ashley told me about his daddy's yacht. Instead, I was checking out the way everyone but the queenliest of queens avoided the Gay & Lesbian stall so as not to give the wrong first impression to potential new best friends. I came away from there feeling that it was just the stereotype of really camp people who were out and proud. I didn't think I was that stereotype so decided I couldn't be gay. However, I was still clearly curious, or perhaps suspicious is a better word as later that term I went to my first gay bar.

One night, whilst out with my housemates going to a new club, I noticed that the club next door was a gay bar. Half way through the night I pretended I wasn't feeling well and left. As I exited the first club I gave a quick glance around to make sure none of my housemates were watching and shot into the gay bar next door. I barely took my eyes off the floor as I fought my way through a mass of eyes, all feeling like they were burrowing into my body. I felt claustrophobic and as I got to the bar I lost my nerve and made a swift exit, receiving a few pats on the arse I as went. I felt so angry when I got out and virtually ran all the way home without looking back. I was angry with myself for not holding myself with more confidence and I was left with the impression that gay bars were full of predators. This put me back on the straight path for quite a few years.

Of course there were crushes and flirtations that, had the other guys been serious, I'm sure I may have been persuaded. The thing is that I didn't know any openly gay guys and it's fair to say that those I thought were obviously gay I avoided, maybe so as not to put temptation at my door or worse still that they'd out me. I couldn't believe I'd managed to blot these things out of my mind. The memories must've been well and truly buried. I again applauded my self-defence mechanism for protecting me.

In fact, the only other real temptation I had was with another woman - my best friend Amanda. We had been so very close for a good few years now and shared everything; definitely soul mates on some level.

How could I tell her about what had happened between Will and I? Should I even tell her? She was the one person I desperately needed to talk to right now, but I decided it would have to wait, pulled the covers over my head and spent pretty much the rest of the day in bed.

Chapter 7

Monday morning arrived after another sleep-starved night. All I'd done was go round and round in circles about whether I was gay or not. Will hadn't called and I was thankful for that, as I couldn't figure out what he meant to me in this big ball of confusion.

I trundled into work and got on with another dull week trying to come up with exciting marketing concepts for wiper blades and the like. I don't know if it was the general discontent I was feeling after the split with Ruth but I was seriously bored with my job. This isn't how my life should be, I was destined for bigger things; I was sure of that. Was now the right time to try and forge a new career though with all that was going on in my head?

The new millennium was just around the corner. If I could just get to the end of the year then I'd go grab life by the balls and make a real go of it next year – new job, new flat…..new sexuality? Ok so I wasn't sure about the last one…how about new love interest? Yep, that's better. Sounds like a Heat magazine headline; *'Has Gary got a new love interest? Find out inside.'* I chuckled to myself at the daydream as Jane appeared beside me.

"What are you laughing at?" she asked with an inquisitive

grin on her face.

"Oh, nothing. Just a little daydream," I said hoping she wouldn't probe further.

"Well I've got something for you to laugh about. It's not even 9.30 and I've already had a classic come through on the customer helpline," said Jane as she pushed aside my file so she could perch on my desk.

"Well.." she began, "so I'm sitting at my desk with my Madonna headset on and the phone goes and no one else is in yet, so I pick up the call..." She dons her posh telephone voice before continuing,

"Good Morning Customer Services how can I help?" "The customer says *'My O Ring is leaking'*. Well, I didn't think I'd heard him right so I say 'Sorry?' and he confirms *'I've got a leaky O Ring.'*"

I couldn't help but laugh, we both knew it was a genuine engine part. Jane managed to carry on,

"You can imagine I couldn't stop from laughing and had to pretend I'd taken a fit of coughing and put it straight through to Thomas who'd just arrived. He says it out loud *'You've got a leaky O Ring?'* and that sets me off even worse. Thomas was struggling to keep a straight face and shooed me off, so here I am. Good night on Saturday wasn't it?" She was on a roll now and didn't even want a response. She leaned in closer and said,

"Listen, I was thinking we need to sort Will out with a boyfriend."

I felt a surprise jealousy rise up in me.

"What do you mean?" I said a bit too harshly making Jane give me a funny look.

"He's such a lovely guy and he shouldn't be single. He needs to get laid. One of my friend's brothers is gay so I thought I'd

35

set them up on a blind date."

She was telling me rather than asking for my opinion, but I couldn't help my knee jerk reaction.

"Are you sure that's a good idea? Maybe Will needs to do this on his own?" I said. Jane was having none of it.

"Jeez, did someone get out the wrong side of bed today?" she said as she whizzed off to find Will.

I took a deep breath. Maybe it would be for the best if Will went on a blind date and found a boyfriend. That way he wouldn't be an option for me and it'd give me space to figure out if I was gay or straight. So why did I feel so jealous? Oh God Jane's telling Will now and he's coming over.

"Morning." he said shyly.

"Hi." I managed back.

"Jane's setting me up on a blind date," he paused, checking no one else was in earshot,

"What do you think I should do? I mean there's what happened the other night and all." Sneaky git. He'd indirectly just asked me what was going on with us and I wasn't sure how to respond. I couldn't stop him from seeing other people, we had no commitments to each other, but I knew I didn't want him to see anyone else just in case I wanted him.

That was too selfish, so I thought I was doing the right thing when I replied,

"You should go for it. It'll be a laugh and good experience if nothing else."

Will looked disappointed with my answer.

"Yeah, I guess you're right. I'll do it then," he said, with the last part sounding more like a question for me to approve, but I wasn't getting fished in. Luckily my phone went at that minute so I had an excuse to get rid of him.

It was my mum. She often rang me at work so I could call her back and save on both our phone bills – she's the thrifty type. She can make one chicken breast feed four people when needs must. I wanted to tell her everything that had happened with Will and Ruth over the weekend and ask for advice, but again I was petrified to even utter the words aloud, not forgetting I was in the middle of an open plan office. I put on my bravest 'I'm fine' voice and let her waffle away about the latest goings on back home.

What I wouldn't have given at that moment to run home to Mum and be a child again, one that didn't have to make big grown up decisions about his life. To have a big hug from her and be told everything would be alright. I put down the phone and tried my best to stop thinking about anything other than a snappy slogan for my next wiper blade promotion *'Wipe your cares away?'* No. *'See more clearly?'* Better. *'Ah wipe your arse for all I care,'* that's the one! Thankfully, the office was closing for Christmas at the end of the week. I don't think I could take much more of this.

Will seemed to keep his distance a little after that day which upset me, but I kept telling myself it was for the best and managed to focus on figuring out those last few Xmas present ideas. At least I wouldn't have to worry about buying for Ruth this year, that'd save me time and money.

I was desperate to know if Will had gone on the blind date but couldn't bring myself to ask him directly, so I casually asked Jane on the last working day before the Christmas holidays.

"Did Will end up going on that blind date?" I asked in a whisper as we stood in the kitchen swigging on the mulled wine that had been provided. Jane did her best spy impression as she pulled me to one corner and said,

"Yes, they went out on Wednesday night, but I don't think it went too well. Will said it went fine but I asked my friend to get the low down from her brother and she said that he thought Will seemed uninterested. Almost as if he had his heart set on someone else?" She paused and let that sink in with me. Surely she didn't know about what happened between Will and I?

"Who?" I asked in my best gossip hungry tone.

"Well, that's just the thing; he didn't say. I think you should ask him."

"Me?!" I gasped.

"Yes, you're good at being upfront and you two have been getting on pretty well of late, so ask him. I bet it's David. Why is it people always want what they can't have?" she said before continuing,

"So that's agreed then, you'll ask him and let me know. Oh there he is now – go for it."

She pushed me towards him as she deposited a cup of mulled wine in my free hand.

"Will, Hi. Mulled wine?" I said, trying to sound as natural as possible, but not knowing how I should act around the guy I had slept with and then pretty much avoided ever since. Will looked a bit suspicious as he accepted the drink without saying anything. He wasn't making this easy for me.

"Had a good week?" I tried.

"Not bad, thanks," was his short answer. I looked round at Jane who was nodding her head, grinning and raising her eyebrows as if to say 'do it!'

I bit the bullet "Jane tells me you went on that blind date on Wednesday. How was that?" I said as casually as possible, but Will just didn't seem to want to play along.

"It was fine. Nice guy but not sure I'll see him again." He said deadpan. The atmosphere felt very frosty as he stared at me and said,

"Well, good to see you Gary but I've got to get on with something before the end of the day." I grabbed his arm.

"Wait! Is there someone else, Will? Is that why you didn't warm to this guy? If it's David, you know you really are wasting your time because..."

"It's not David!" he said angrily, and then his face softened as he saw the sadness in my eyes.

"Look, it's no one. Have a good Christmas yeah, and maybe see you when you get back from Hampshire?"

"Yeah, that'd be good. In fact I was going to have a new year's party if you're around?" I offered feeling a yearning to make him smile.

"Oh, I can't. It's my dad's 60th and we're all going out for that." He said looking genuinely disappointed, before adding, "Leave it with me. I might be able to come a bit later than midnight." With that he was gone and I went to report back to Jane that it wasn't David.

I guess I'd deserved Will's coldness, but it left me feeling scolded and yearning for him, wanting to be near him and hold him. Shit! I was falling for him wasn't I?

Chapter 8

hristmas in Hampshire with the family was a quiet affair. The whole family were still treating me with kid gloves since I'd split up with Ruth and I was beginning to climb the walls and crave my life in London. I made my getaway on the 28th December telling a little white lie that I had a friend's birthday to attend.

Before I knew it, it was the eve of the new millennium and in some ways I did feel as if the world had ended. I'd been so caught up in trying not to think about the split with Ruth and the fact that I was becoming more convinced that I was gay. Everywhere I'd been in the last couple of weeks I'd been looking at men and women and deciding if I fancied them. The men were winning hands down with very few women doing it for me. All December, I'd been partying hard and was only too glad of another excuse to party like it was 1999, which it just so happened to be. I invited my best friend Amanda, Jane and five other pals over to my flat to see in the New Year.

We were getting more and more drunk and playing drinking games as the clock edged ever closer to midnight. At around 23.40 we headed out into the town centre to join the throng of revellers who had flocked out of the pubs and clubs to stand on the street and shout the countdown from ten seconds to midnight and welcome in the new millennium.

Our group stood in a circle in the middle of the crowded High Street as the chants went out… *ten!*…I felt excited …*nine!* ..then realisation struck me ….*eight!* …*seven!* ….*six!*….*five!*…I felt like I couldn't breathe….*four!*….*three!*….got to get out of here *two!*….*one!*.. *"May old acquaintance be forgot."* I could feel the sting of tears on my hot cheeks as I pushed my way through the crowd back towards my flat. I'd been focusing on making it through to the end of the year for a fresh start; now it was here and the bottled up emotion had exploded like the corks on the champagne bottles being popped all around the country. The sheer panic of 'Now what?' hit me.

Amanda was the first to find me lying on the floor at the side of my bed sobbing.

"Please. Just leave me a while. I'll be ok. I don't want to ruin it for everyone else." I managed to spit out before she could say anything. She looked at me with pity, but understood that she must step in and entertain the others until I got it together. About twenty minutes later the bedroom door opened and I was surprised to see Will with a Kiss Me Quick hat on. He'd been at his Dad's 60th birthday party (hence the hat), and I'd completely forgotten that I'd invited him to my New Years' get together. I didn't want him seeing me like this but it was too late.

"Gary, what's up?" he asked, concerned. I put on my bravest face.

"I'll be ok, it's just been a hard few months and when the bells tolled it kind of all just came out." I replied. Will looked shiftily around, then seeing that we were alone gave me a long lingering kiss. I suddenly felt completely happy in that moment. Will and I had such a great chemistry and I wanted to hold on to that instant forever. However, none of the other party guests knew about us and I was soon pushing him away for fear of being caught mid kiss.

"Go get me a drink. It's New Year and we need to celebrate. I'm just going to go powder my nose," I said as I went to the bathroom.

As I looked at my tear stained face in the mirror, I had a moment of clarity. I knew that I was a good person with a big heart and that my life was mine to mould. I also thought that I was gay and with that would come many challenging times ahead. For now I had a party animal reputation to uphold; my problems could wait for another day.

We partied until the small hours and when it came time for bed Will hit the sofa, whilst Amanda shared my double bed. I lay there waiting for her to nod off and then I snuck into the sitting room and saw the New Year in with a different kind of bang with Will. We had to be so silent, but that just added to the passion. Afterwards I snuck back in the bedroom, leaving Amanda none the wiser.

Next morning, I awoke with a genuine smile on my face. It had been a tough year and now here we were at the start of a new one; a fresh start. Amanda was already up and making bacon sandwiches as she chatted to Will. As I walked in he gave me a big grin which I couldn't help but reciprocate. The electricity in the air was palpable and as soon as Amanda went to shower, Will was all over me, hands and lips frantically grabbing and kissing. But then I heard the shower turn off I had to push him away and try to focus on the news to turn off my dirty mind.

Amanda and I were spending the day together so Will got showered and dressed and left, making the 'call me' sign with his hand when Amanda wasn't looking.

"You alright Gary?" asked Amanda the minute we'd closed the door and sat down with a cuppa.

"Yes. I'm feeling good, I think the new millennium is going to be…interesting" I replied.

I saw Will again the next night and the next and the next, but didn't tell anyone. There was a naughtiness in the secrecy of our meet ups and excitement at being in the first stages of a potential relationship. It had been over seven years since I'd had the rush of wanting to be with someone every waking minute. Wanting to know all about them, discovering your mutual loves and hates, and of course there was the sex; we were horny all the time. I was desperately trying not to rush into anything either, fully aware that I'd not long come out of a long term relationship. However, I also knew that I'm an all or nothing kind of guy with very little patience. I'd thrown myself head first into what was only supposed to be a bit of fun.

Chapter 9

After Christmas, I started back to work and as the weeks progressed Will and I were getting more and more daring with each other; sitting with our hands held under the desk or me rubbing Will's leg with my foot as we discussed important sales figures. I'm sure our flirtatious doe-eyed looks at each other weren't going unnoticed by colleagues, but none of them would have ever been bold enough to suspect that we were anything other than friends. This was an automotive manufacturer. The type of people who worked here were mostly mechanics or nerds. The sales guys were typical lads and the customers were often Joe Bloggs Garage in deepest, darkest Grimsby. I remember going on a couple of customer visits and the machismo just oozes out of every workshop, which are often decorated with various Page 3 Girl calendars. This was not an industry for being gay or even slightly effeminate. I had the advantage of having two older brothers so could turn on my inner lad when needed, but I knew that I couldn't keep living a lie. I had to get a new job in a new industry; one that excited me.

One day I was feeling so naughty that I followed Will into the toilet and pushed him into the cubicle nearest the wall and started to kiss him against his muffled protests. Then we heard the door open and recognised the voices of several colleagues. I had to put my hand to my mouth to suppress a giggle. Will looked panicked but there was nothing we could do; or was there? I decided that if we were going to be stuck in there a while that I'd have to take matters into hand and maybe my mouth as well. The joy of the seduction is that Will couldn't say anything. I fought hard to hold in my laugh as Will looked like an insane mime trying to get me to stop, but I soon won him over and he stood in silence, whilst I pleasured him. When the job was done we noticed that there was silence in the room so Will flushed the loo and tentatively walked out of the cubicle but stopped half in half out. The Sales Manager (Will's boss) was stood at the urinal round the corner.

"Ah Will, there you are. Wondered where you'd got too. You around for a quick catch up?" He said.

"Yeah sure," replied Will, pale with the fear of getting sprung.

"You alright Will? You don't look so good." said his boss.

"Oh I've just had a bit of an upset stomach," Will invented as another colleague came in and went to go in the cubicle where I was still hiding.

"Don't go in there!" said Will in panic.

His boss used his salesman charm to back him up. "Yeah, Will's just lost half his guts in there." At which, the newcomer swiftly chose the cubicle next to me and I breathed a huge sigh of relief as Will and his boss left the room and I was able to sneak out. That was too close for comfort.

After that near miss, Will was never the same at work and I struggled with it. Outside of work in the secrecy of our homes, he couldn't keep his hands off me and was very loving, but now, at work, every move I made was met with resistance. I felt a bit rejected by this and it further fuelled me in my desire to get out of this job and move into something that interested me. I started applying for jobs in the entertainment industry.

* * *

Another change was more imminent as it had come time for me to leave the flat that Ruth and I had shared for over two years. I never thought I'd be leaving it without her. In fact, I thought we'd be getting a mortgage and moving into our first owned-home together; where we'd start a family. The children would almost certainly be chubby babies with dark curly hair if our baby photos were anything to go on. I realised that being gay would mean that I might never have children of my own. At 23, I was definitely too young to want kids right now, but I think I'd always been brought up to be family focused and so children were always in my future plans. I brushed the realisation from my mind as I did my last walk round the flat, the memories of the happy times Ruth and I'd had appeared liked ghosts in front of my eyes.

What was I doing? She was a lovely girl and we'd had good times. Maybe it wasn't too late to sort things out and get back together with her? It'd be like having a little break from each other so that we could step back and realise what was truly important and be happy ever after in our society approved relationship complete with a man, a woman, a wedding and 2.4 children.

I was the most mixed up I'd ever been. I had to shake myself. Ruth and I were over and this was best for both of us. I was free.

I'd been a serial monogamist for a year and a half before Ruth with only a short gap before getting together with her. After seven years together, I had missed out on the pulling in pubs and clubs and the one-night stands and being able to go out with your pals without having to check in with someone else first. I had so much to catch up on. Saying that, didn't I sort of have an other-half again in Will? Clearly, some habits are hard to break.

My focus shifted to him now as I looked at the bed where he'd been staying with more frequency. What was I doing? Was it just the sex? The company? I didn't like to admit it but I was desperately lonely since Ruth and I had split up and when no one was around to keep me entertained, I would start feeling very sorry for myself. I think I was avoiding being on my own so I didn't have to think about my feelings and sort myself out.

It was more than that though, it was as if my life plan had somehow been screwed up and thrown in the bin and now I was staring at a blank canvas, unsure what to paint. I couldn't get my head to believe that I was lucky having such freedom. The world should have been my oyster now. I had no ties and there was no rush either. I could do whatever I liked, whenever I liked, with whomever I liked - I only had to explain my actions to myself. If I could live with what I was doing and no one was getting hurt then what was the problem? But clearly there was a problem, as rather than embrace the opportunity I was a little lost lamb, questioning my every move.

I was afraid and needed to hear that it didn't matter if I was, in fact, gay. That I was a good person who would find a new job and my friends and family would still love me. I had lots of friends, but I'd only told Will about my feelings of being gay. I hadn't even told my best friend Amanda. I told her everything and was feeling guilty about keeping this to myself. Amanda had offered me her spare room whilst I found another place to rent, so that's where I was heading now.

I wiped the tears from my eyes which had been quietly winding their way down my cheeks and said goodbye to Flat 24 and to the good and the bad times that I'd had there. I posted the keys through the letterbox and carried the final bag down to the car.

Amanda lived about a thirty minute drive away, but that car journey seemed to go on for about three hours. Every radio station seemed to be playing songs about love lost and being alone, even the tape I had in the car was taunting me as it played Steps' *After the Love Has Gone.* Listening to Steps - another sign that I was a bona fide gay perhaps?

My mind was working overtime and once again I thought my head might just explode there and then in the car and what a mess that'd make on the windscreen. I was more changeable than the British weather – one minute thinking that I should make a play to get back with Ruth and the next that I should just play the field and be single and see which sex I was ultimately attracted to. Of course there was Will to think about too. I think I was quite smitten with him already, but was trying to play it cool as this wasn't supposed to be anything other than a bit of fun. I don't know what he was feeling about the whole thing and dared not ask him for fear of his reply. I didn't really want to hear that he was head over heels in love with me anymore than I wanted to hear it was only a fling and nothing serious.

A car horn nudged me on at the traffic lights where I'd drifted off into my troubled thoughts. I wasn't far from Amanda's now so I needed to get it together. I wiped my eyes as gently as I could and pulled my best fake smile. I started my pep talk,

'You're young, ok looking, hard working, have some savings and a well enough paid job – you can do whatever you want to do.' It was working somewhat as I chanted the last bit over and over again like an American motivational speaker. I could still hear the nagging voice of doubt in my head *'but what is it that you want to do Gary? And is it girls or boys you want?'* I just chanted my mantra louder and louder until I found other drivers looking at me strangely as if I was deranged or possibly angry with them for some reason.

I pulled up to Amanda's place, took a few deep breaths and put on my pretend happy face as I carried my bags to her house. She was waiting at the door with a beam on her face that was pure excitement.

"Hello, hello!" she chirped.

"All done? Good. I'm looking forward to having you here. It'll be like old times eh? Although don't forget we are older now. Don't know about wiser, but we shouldn't have impromptu parties on Sundays. I don't think I could make it into work with a hangover anymore." I was desperately trying to share her enthusiasm but all those suppressed worries and thoughts suddenly boiled over and I burst into tears.

"Hey, hey it's alright. Aw come here love." Amanda was the person I needed right now. She pulled me to her and gently patted my back as I sobbed on her shoulder. I'd cried a lot over the last few months and Amanda had borne most of the brunt of that too, but I still felt a twinge of embarrassment and pulled away taking lots of those big huffy puffy sighs you do when you're trying to stop yourself crying. Amanda gave me a box of tissues and ushered me to the sofa.

"You're bound to feel emotional so don't be embarrassed. Let it all out, that's what I always say." She had a mumsy feel about her that was so welcoming and calming too.

"I'll go and make us a cup of tea. I assume a cake wouldn't go a miss or are you too upset for a Viennese Whirl?" she teased.

"Oh I'll give it a go." I snivelled "Got to keep my strength up." I even managed a laugh.

Silly fool, I thought to myself. Why are you getting yourself all upset? You'll be fine. You've got Amanda's to stay at until you find another place, you'll have a right laugh. Just give yourself time to think things through and stop putting pressure on yourself all the time.

"There you go," said Amanda as she handed me my tea and cake.

"Thanks Mand. You're the best," I mumbled through a mouthful of cake.

"Yeah I know. Now what has set you off today?" she asked.

"I think it was just the finality of leaving the flat. Even though Ruth's not been there for a few months it seems to have made it more real that we've split up." I paused and stared off into space. I was thinking out loud and Amanda was a great one for encouraging this and giving the appropriate time and cues to 'get it all out' as she'd said. I continued,

"I thought I was over the split. We both know that I was devastated at first, but once I'd gotten over the shock I realised it was what I wanted too." I slurped some tea before going on,

"I guess that today brought back all the memories and made me feel like I really was closing the door on that part of my life."

"Well, you know what they say," said Amanda

"Yeah, yeah, I know one door closes another one opens." I interrupted.

"No, I was going to say you're better off without the old

witch." She said and started belly laughing – she was always laughing at her own jokes. I think she surprised herself at how funny she could be sometimes. I think her sense of humour was one of the reasons I got on so well with her.

The mood was lifted and I didn't want to return to analysing my thoughts so we had what we knew we shouldn't – an impromptu party; even though it was Sunday. The alcohol flowed and the dancing began in the dining room, with the table pushed back to the side of the room to allow us to strut our funky stuff to DJ Luck and MC Neat, Britney Spears and All Saints. We had a great night and didn't discuss my problems at all. Every time I felt them resurface I'd just dance harder or get another drink. That night the alcohol made me go out like a light; a trick I was beginning to master and one that worried me slightly too – I didn't want to add alcoholic to my list of issues. I managed to sleep through until about 3am when I had to run to the bathroom and be sick. I thought that Viennese Whirl had tasted a bit off!

* * *

I knew when I first met Amanda that we would be great friends. We met at an interview day for our placement year at university. She was slightly older than most of the other candidates, about 5ft with long curly blond hair that resembled a judges wig. She was from Manchester and seemed very smiley and friendly; full of self-confidence. I don't recall seeing much of her during the day as we were split into separate groups. The thing that sticks in my mind (and why I knew we'd be friends if we both got the jobs) is at the end of the day I randomly sat next to Amanda and whilst making small talk, another potential applicant was holding court. She had a mouth the size of the Grand Canyon and clearly wasn't shy of using it. As she let out an amazingly banal question, I looked at Amanda and we both rolled our eyes; I realised she didn't suffer fools either.

I thought I'd done quite well at the Assessment Day, though you can never tell with these things. I'm not very good at blagging so instead just try to be myself and be philosophical about the outcome – i.e. what you see is what you get and if you like me, you offer me the job, if you don't like me, then your loss (and then I have a hissy fit about why they didn't want me). In this case I was right; I got offered one of ten placements and was sent a pack with contact information of the nine other students who'd be joining me on my placement year. As I scanned down the list I recognised Amanda's name and chuckled to myself about the moment we had shared at the end of the assessment day.

That summer we ended up moving into a house together with two other placement students and I had one of the best years of my life.

As I suspected, we clicked instantly. We did flirt a lot, but I was with Ruth from the beginning and although Amanda was single, it was never anything more than pals having a laugh with each other. In fact, all four of us flirted with each other and wound each other up even though we were two guys and two girls; it was all just harmless banter. Amanda did have a couple of flings that year but they didn't go beyond the placement year and she remained single.

We stayed in touch and visited each other after we returned for our final year at university and I was delighted when I learned that we'd both gotten our first jobs post graduating on the outskirts of London. Prior to moving in with her now, we had the kind of relationship where we saw each other on a regular basis and were constantly emailing and calling each other. She confided in me and I in her. She just seemed to get me, like I said we were soul mates on some level. Looking back, I didn't even think how Ruth must've felt about me having a close friend who was female. I don't think I'd be too happy with her having a male best friend who took on some of the role that I would expect to play.

As I started the next phase of my life, Amanda was just the tonic I needed and living with her seemed to be going great. She seemed to be enjoying having me around as well and I was faintly aware of a new optimism in her. I actually found I was shutting out the problems in my mind and living in a bit of a Gary and Amanda bubble. Sure, we'd get up and go to work, but then when we got home we'd chat the night away, go for a drink; we even started jogging (that was short lived). To all intents and purposes we were a couple. She'd replaced Ruth and I'd given her the companion I think she desperately wanted in her life. The only thing missing was the sex but we often had a hug and played with each other's hair as we sat watching Coronation Street.

The only thing threatening to break up our slightly dysfunctional cohabiting was Will. I still hadn't told Amanda about what had already happened with Will, let alone that I thought I might be gay. It was strange but I didn't really think of Will as a guy, he was just the person I was falling for. It's almost as if I didn't see it as being gay. I think that was how I made it possible for me to deal with it. Amanda knew that Will and I had been seeing a lot more of each other of late, but then she knew that I was seeing a lot of all my friends since splitting from Ruth. In fact she often told me off for it because she could see that I was just trying to avoid being alone and not allowing myself time to enjoy my own company.

She had been single for many years and had lived on her own for the last couple of years so had gotten used to being on her own, although, even in the year we lived together previously, she always liked having time out on her own.

I think I'd purposely pushed Will away slightly that first couple of weeks living with Amanda. I didn't want to think about him or anything to ruin the comfy bubble I was living in. I couldn't run forever though. I missed his touch and yearned to hear his voice and find out what he was up to. He had been up and down the country on business too so I hadn't seen him in the office either. I'd arranged to meet him on Saturday night and told Amanda that I'd stay at his as we were going out clubbing in London with some of his pals. She looked a little bit hurt that she wasn't being invited along and then caught herself and said nonchalantly,

"It'll be good to get rid of you for a night and get my place back to myself," which hurt me a little as it reminded me that our living arrangement was only temporary.

Off I went to spend the night with Will. I felt so nervous as I rang the bell of his flat. He looked a mixture of excited and nervous too as he opened the door wearing an oven glove.

"Hi," he said and kissed me on the cheek as I walked into the flat shutting the door from prying eyes. "I thought I'd just cook and we'd stay in and watch a video instead. That ok?" he continued. I pushed him hard against the wall and kissed him deeply.

"Mmmm, that sounds fine to me." I kissed him again "I've missed you" I blurted out and saw the shock register on his face. Shit! Why had I said that, he'll think I'm too full on, he'll think that…my thoughts were interrupted by him pushing me back against the opposite wall and kissing me slow and delicately.

"I've missed you too" he said moving my hand to his groin.

"I can feel that!" I laughed and started to go for his zip.

"Ah ah, all in good time. I've got to impress you with my culinary skills first. Now go and sit down. Glass of wine?" asked Will as he disappeared into the kitchen. Before I had chance to reply he came out with a glass of Chardonnay in his hand and kissed me again before placing the wine glass into my hand and ushering me to the living room. Luckily his flat was of an era that he actually still had a serving hatch between the kitchen and living room so he was able to talk to me whilst putting together a Thai red curry with rice.

As the curry needed time to simmer away, Will suggested we walk to Blockbuster video and hire a DVD for the night. When we arrived, Will seemed a little tentative when it came to picking a film. I don't know whether he didn't want me to question his taste or was merely trying to be polite and let the guest pick. I had no qualms in saying what I liked and didn't like, but obviously wanted to find out more about Will and asked him what were his biggest film turn offs.

"Well, I'm not really into musicals or animation. And without wishing to sound prudey, I don't really like a lot of swearing." He said.

Generally speaking I agreed with those taste choices, however I noticed South Park: Bigger, Longer, Uncut was out on DVD and having loved it at the cinema, persuaded Will to trust me on hiring it. We also picked up some lemon cheesecake flavoured Häagen-Dazs ice cream.

We had a fantastic couply night in with delicious food, good wine, easy conversation and despite his reservations, Will thoroughly enjoyed the South Park movie. Then there was the afters. Any fear of me thinking I was gay, was far from my mind as we did what lovers do. It just felt so right, completely natural and fantastically exciting.

The next day we spent the morning in bed only to be interrupted by Amanda phoning to ask if I'd be home for Sunday lunch. We hadn't realised the time but it had gone past noon and so I got up to shower and then I did something I would live to regret. I told Will I loved him as I kissed him goodbye. I didn't see the fear in his eyes as I walked away deliriously happy again, something I didn't think I would be just six months after the split with Ruth.

* * *

Amanda was acting a little strange when I got home and seemed a bit narky and short tempered. Something was clearly bothering her and I didn't know what it was but even her moodiness couldn't ruin my euphoria – I was in love. I had to tell her about me and Will.

That night we had another impromptu party because I thought she needed cheering up. It was Sunday but she had the Monday off work so didn't need too much encouragement and I had no scruples. We got the wine and crisps out and put on Beautiful South and Spice Girl CDs and got silly drunk and danced the evening away. It was about eleven when we decided we'd best turn the music down for the sake of the neighbours and sat down to another glass of wine and began putting the world to rights. She had been narky because she was sick of being single and was asking me if there was something wrong with her. I reassured her that she was fantastic and that there is a great bloke out there for her but she needs to help herself by getting out there more to find him.

She got bored of talking about herself and asked me what had put me in such a good mood.

"Did you meet someone last night at the club?" She looked almost relieved when I replied,

"No." I expanded "I didn't go clubbing last night," not making eye contact and feeling like I was revealing a naughty secret. Amanda was going to love this. It was gossip of the juiciest kind. I continued,

"Will cooked and we just stayed in and watched a video." Amanda was looking quizzically at me.

"I've been kind of seeing him for a couple of months now. We're going out." I finished and looked up expecting to see her excited face telling me off for keeping something from me for so long. She looked shell shocked.

"I'm…I'm just going to the toilet," she said and walked off like a zombie. I sat there nervously going over recent events in my mind. Amanda returned her face heavy with worry.

"That wasn't quite the reaction I was hoping for chick?" I said but she didn't flinch.

"I'm a bit shocked really Gary," she said. She never used my name unless it was serious.

"So are you telling me you are gay now? How long have you known that?" The last part sounded quite accusative.

"I don't really know what's going on if I'm honest, only that I think I'm in love with him," I said with the last bit trailing off slightly as if I felt ashamed for saying it.

"How can you be in love? You've only just split up with Ruth. You're just a bit confused poppet." Amanda said in what seemed like a concerned way that I found very patronising. I finally thought I was getting somewhere in my head and now she was reminding me how ridiculous the whole thing sounded. I wasn't in love with Will, I was in love with the idea of being in love with him. Not to say that we wouldn't both be in love in a couple of months' time but it doesn't just happen overnight.

"I can't really explain it…and I don't want to!" I snapped. "I'm happy, can't you just be happy for me?"

"Alright, calm down, calm down" said Amanda in her best impression of the Scousers from Harry Enfield. It instantly lightened the mood.

"Sorry. I know you're only looking out for me and I know you're right but after all I went through splitting up with Ruth, I just want to let this go wherever it wants to go." I said.

"So you're saying you're definitely gay?" asked Amanda and I felt a surge of panic.

"I don't know what I am. I feel like I'm falling for a guy so maybe I'm bi-sexual?"

"Have you ever felt like this with another guy?"

"Well I have sort of messed around with another guy when I was younger, but doesn't everyone experiment? It wasn't a passionate thing, more practical."

"I know that they say that, but I'm not sure how many guys I've met that have. Maybe they're just not admitting it? Anyway, like you say, you could be bi-sexual. Either way I want you to think really carefully about Will and try not to rush in to anything. When I met you, you were with Ruth and you've never really allowed yourself to just be on your own. I'm not saying split up with Will, but if it fizzles out, I really think it would be a good idea just to be on your own for a while. You know, get your head straight."

I felt suddenly sober despite all the wine and now my

head, which had felt settled, was off on a rollercoaster ride of questioning my sexuality and my recent actions. I gave Amanda a big hug and made my way to bed feigning tiredness.

In the middle of the night, I was sick out of my bedroom window onto the garden path, not with worry but with wine I'm sorry to say – would I ever learn?

Next morning wasn't a pretty sight and I had to clear it up whilst trying not to be sick again. To my surprise Amanda was up and gave me a big hug and a bit of a pep talk before I left the house. I was too tired to argue back so I let her have her say; she was just being protective of me like she always was.

"You might be making a big mistake. You're on the rebound and you're very vulnerable, and some things have happened, but try not to read too much into them. You are very needy at the moment, and when someone shows you affection you probably find it really welcoming. Don't just jump from one bad relationship to another. Give yourself time to be on your own and to think things through properly. Nothing that you've done has to be permanent, you're in a fragile state whether you think so or not so no one will be offended if you feel you have to go back on things that have happened." I fobbed off her speech by telling her I would think about it all and not make any quick decisions.

My day had not started well and it was going to get worse. Amanda's speech had gotten to me because I felt like she was telling me that I should end things with Will and I didn't like being told what to do.

Work was incredibly busy and I had a delayed hangover that kicked in about 11am and lasted throughout the day. As I left work a broken man, I was lifted at the sight of Will in the car park. He was clearly waiting for me and this made my heart flutter, I was definitely feeling the love bug no matter what Amanda thought. As I got closer I noticed that Will was looking really nervous and not making eye contact with me.

"Hey Honey, ten dollar, love you long time?" I joked but I could see instantly that this wasn't the time for jokes. Will looked really uncomfortable.

"What's up?" I said and put my hand on his shoulder. He jerked it away and looked round to make sure no one saw.

"Look Gary, I'm sorry but I don't think we should see each other anymore." He said without making eye contact. He looked like he was about to cry yet I was the one getting dumped again for the second time in six months.

"But why?" I asked.

"What's happened?"

Will ummed and arred for a while and said,

"I just don't know that I can give you what you need. I really like you and it's been fun, but I think you want more out of this than I can give you so I think it's best to end it now, before it goes too far." I was not going to cry in front of him.

I was so angry.

"This is because of what I said to you as I left yesterday isn't it? I didn't mean that…well I sort of meant it. I just got carried away." I said.

Will couldn't look at me.

"Oh forget it! Good night Will." I stomped off to my car, with Will calling after me. I just ignored him and drove home seething and with my head still throbbing.

As I drove further away from work my anger dissipated and I began to think back to what Amanda had said to me that morning. I felt a strange lack of emotion about Will, it had been a shitty day and I'd slipped into a neutral state that if I'd been told my whole family had been killed I think I'd have replied 'That's a shame'. I was floating outside my body and feeling no emotions. Will dumping me was actually a kind of blessing today as it took out one of my options. My thoughts then turned to Amanda and why she'd acted out of character both last night and this morning with her pushy advice. What was she playing at? Then it suddenly dawned on me – she fancied me, she must do. She had reacted so badly to the news of Will and I being together. Could she have been hoping that she and I would get together when Ruth and I split up?

Amanda and I, a couple? I let the thought resonate in my head. I'd never really considered it, yet it made so much sense. We got on really well; I can't remember ever having an argument and she laughed at all my jokes. She'd met my family and got on with them and I'd met hers. Could it be that the answer was right under my nose the whole time (and not just because of her height). I already loved her as my best friend and I'm sure the attraction could develop if I let it. Screw Will. He'd been a mistake. Amanda was right, he just came along at a time when I needed someone and he got lucky. It could've been anyone girl or guy, plus I was feeling rebellious after splitting from Ruth and wanted to try the gay thing. It was a phase; just a phase.

I rushed home with a second wind keen to see Amanda. My headache had even subsided slightly. I persuaded Amanda that I was feeling a lot clearer in my head and wanted to take her to dinner to thank her. We had a great night and I found myself falling for the idea of us being a couple. So much so that on the way home I suggested we sit down and look at the stars. It was then that I decided to tell her that I thought we should get together and kissed her. She didn't resist and we rushed home in silence anticipating what was to follow. I was feeling very nervous. Was I doing the right thing or was I just rebounding from Ruth to Will and now to Amanda? When we got home she started kissing me passionately and undoing my shirt. I was kissing her back, but in my mind's eye I had an image of Will looking at me saying *"What are you doing?"* I couldn't do this, it wasn't right. I didn't love Amanda in that way. I pulled away and slid down the wall in tears, apologising to Amanda. She walked out of the room and I thought I'd blown it. Not only had I lost my girlfriend and my sort of boyfriend, but now I had screwed things up with my best friend too.

To my surprise Amanda came back in again with mascara running down her face and two cups of tea. She slumped up against the wall next to me and handed me my tea. We looked at each other and laughed – we were both tear stained and what a mess. I gave her a big hug.

"I'm so sorry Amanda. I love you to bits, but I think I really am gay." I said, in a moment of clarity.

"I know. To be honest, I always had my suspicions but you're such a lovely guy and you'd be a perfect husband. My perfect husband!" She said and punched me.

"Why did you have to be gay?"

"Well, who else would you go shopping with?" I retorted nudging her back and we both laughed.

"You're a crap kisser anyway. It'd never work" she jested. We laughed and hugged.

"I'm sorry I was a bit of a bitch about Will. He's a lovely guy and you two make a good couple if I let myself even think of you with another man," she said feigning indignation.

"Well I'm sorry love but you'll have to take your new hat back because the weddings off. He dumped me today". I sighed.

"Aw Love, well that's his loss. Just wait until the gay world hears you've switched sides they'll be knocking down the door." Amanda ruffled my hair in a motherly way.

"Come on let's go to bed…. Separately I should add. Unless you want to give it one more go?" she winked.

What a day it had been. I felt the sorrow of losing Will coming over me as I went to bed. If Amanda couldn't make me want to be with a girl I'd just have to face facts…I was gay. Gay and heartbroken already; oh the drama of it all – maybe I would be good at this gay thing after all.

Chapter 10

How much had I drunk last night? I couldn't move, my head was thumping and my legs felt like lead. Last night's events replayed in my mind. What a fool I'd been and how badly had I messed Amanda around lately. She'd been great; I wish I had her strength, especially now when I needed every ounce of mine to get me to the shower.

On my third attempt I managed to lift my head and chest off the bed and push up onto my knees where I waited for a wave of nausea to pass before I attempted to stand. Like man landing on the moon I took each step in tentative slow motion as the room seemed to be made of rubber; contorting around me and throwing me off balance. With the aid of the walls I managed to stagger to the bathroom and turn on the shower. Self pity would be my only friend today. I was suffering physically and emotionally. The hangover was merely pushing me further into 'Woe is me' territory as I kept thinking *'what's wrong with me? Why doesn't Will want me?'* I wanted to curl up in the shower and cry all day, but I didn't even have the strength to do that. After a very long shower, I managed to get dressed and sip some tea before making my way out to catch the train.

The fresh air was chilly but strangely refreshing, giving me the boost I needed to walk at a slightly faster than geriatric pace (I know this to be true as I overtook old Mrs Higgins from down the road and it was neck and neck there for a while). I was feeling like the nausea had subsided and the paracetamol were kicking in to stop the tom tom players in my head beating their erratic rhythm. The next obstacle was a 30 minute train ride. This was to prove an unpleasant experience for both me and my fellow travellers.

I picked up a free Metro newspaper and took a seat where I felt least likely to be disturbed by cheery commuters. I put my iPod on quietly with some mellow music and tried to read, but that just brought back the wobble vision that I'd had in the bedroom that morning. Ok I'll just take deep breaths and look out the window. To the rest of the train I must've looked like I was an expectant mother practising my lemans breathing but, in an out of character moment, I couldn't care less what they thought of me; I had to focus on not being sick on the train. The sweats were coming now along with a watery mouth. Come on. Come on! I urged the train to arrive at my stop. I was feeling the panic now, where was the toilet on this train? Could I make it? I went to stand and realised that was not going to help, so I bent in two and concentrated harder than I'd ever done before on my breathing.

'The next station is Kensington Olympia.' The tanoy announced. Hallelujah! I'm going to make it and I can discreetly be sick in one of the bins or flower beds. Scrap that, I'm not going to make it: I'm going to be sick any second now. *Improvise! The paper, use the paper!* It was like an inner voice guiding me as my fuddled brain slowly realised what I had to do. I made a cone shape with the paper and buried my head in the top trying to be sick as quietly as possible. I was suddenly aware of my fellow passengers' disgust and I couldn't blame them. The shame was engulfing me as I got up swiftly to leave the train holding the offending newspaper cone tightly. A little too tightly it turns out. As I got off the train the cone collapsed and my own vomit gushed down my trouser leg. I rushed to the toilet and did the best I could to clean myself up. I got many strange looks as I stood there in my boxer shorts, holding my damp trousers under the hand dryer – it must've looked like I had pissed myself, which right now I was thinking mightn't have been so bad. I was glad that this was an out of office meeting and not my regular commute otherwise I would have had to quit my job: I couldn't face seeing all those people on the train every day, knowing they'd seen me with my own vomit trickling down my leg.

I sneaked out of the toilets and hung my head in shame as I walked the final part of the journey. That sickly feeling had all but gone and was soon replaced with dread: Will was going to be at the meeting too.

The last time we talked, he told me we were just a bit of fun and that we should stop seeing each other for my own benefit. Cheek of it, what did he care about what I wanted? I wanted to be with him and live in a big castle by the sea. I wanted happily ever after. He was being selfish and I felt used and tossed aside. Since he'd dumped me I had rushed home, drunk copious amounts of alcohol, decided I was straight and tried to cop off with my best friend, then been sick on the train and on my trousers by deflection. I was in no mood to be greeted by him in the client's doorway with,

"Hi Gary. You feeling alright you look a little off colour?" I gave him a hurt look and said,

"I think I'm coming down with that bug that's going around and I didn't get much sleep last night." He looked guilty as sin and awkwardly sat back down. Bill was there too and chipped in,

"Yeah there's a lot of it going around at the moment. Kelly is off with it this week and Shane had it the week before." Well at least I had a cover story.

Throughout the morning I felt the rage and misery taking turns to play with me. Every time Will spoke, or I looked at him, I'd either want to cry or punch him – sometimes both. *"Why did you do that to me, what is wrong with me?"* screamed my inner voice.

I was imagining in my head a scene that made me look like all those hard done by insecure women in rom-coms. Oh my gosh, I had to be gay if I was imagining myself in the form of Julia Roberts or Sandra Bullock.

I could see that Will was really uncomfortable around me the whole day too. He kept going to put his arm around me or touch my shoulder and then bottling it and so it looked like he had some weird tick. He would also open his mouth as if he was going to say something and then Bill would walk back in and he'd just whistle or say something inane like, *'Lovely fresh day today.'*

I was really grateful that the meeting finished early and I was free to go home at 4pm. As I was getting my stuff together Will came over and said,

"We need to talk. Can I give you a lift home?" Not now, Will. He really did have a bad way with timing. Before I had time to respond Bill called him over.

"Will, have you got 10 minutes to go through some of the figures we discussed today?"

Will had to accept. I got my composure back and mumbled, "Thanks anyway, but I'll just get the train." then disappeared faster than a line of coke at an ageing rockstar's party.

The journey home was a greatly improved one to the way into work and luckily I didn't see any of my fellow commuters from that morning. Yet again I found myself void of emotions as sheer exhaustion took hold. I started to laugh at myself; what a day it had been.

By the time I got home the tiredness was taking over. I ran myself a nice hot bath pulling a flannel over my weary eyes and went into a state of suspended animation, only to be awoken by the doorbell. I was going to ignore it, but it rang again and again so I thought it must be Amanda and she'd forgotten her keys. I clambered out of the bath and wrapped a towel around my waist.

"Alright, alright I'm coming hold your horses." I shouted, as I walked to the door.

"Did you forget your….keys?" The latter part of the sentence was barely above a whisper as I opened the door.

"Oh it's you." I said, in shock.

"Can I come in?" said Will.

"Erm…sure. I'll just go get dressed" I said in a bit of a panic.

"Actually, I'd prefer it if you didn't," he said with a cheeky grin on his face. I tried to look unimpressed.

What was he playing at? Was he thinking that we'd discussed it only being fun and now he thought I was some sort of booty call until he found somebody better?

"I'll go get ready. Stick the kettle on would you." I said over my shoulder as I went upstairs.

I sat down on the bed and just stared at myself in the mirror, what was going on? I gave myself a pep talk about being strong and holding it together.

I threw on my slouch pants and a baggy jumper as if to prove to myself that I wasn't making any special effort for Will. He was nervous as he handed me my tea. I eyed him suspiciously and purposely made my way to the single seat rather than sit next to him on the sofa. I could tell that had thrown him.

His eyes were looking upward as he was clearly running through some rehearsed speech in his head.

"How did you think the meeting went today?" he asked. I was thrown by this and instantly blurted out,

"Couldn't this have waited til the office tomorrow?"

Will looked ashamed as his head lowered, eyes finding something interesting on the floor.

"Sorry. We both know that's not why I'm here." Will said before pausing a little.

"I think I've made a mistake" he said. I wanted it spelt out to me.

"Think?!" I shouted.

"I have made a mistake." He said sheepishly.

"And what is that?" I prompted. He clearly wasn't ready to cut to the chase, but insisted on going into his rehearsed monologue; the one he must've been working out in the car on the way over I imagined.

"Today's meeting was horrible. I could see that you were upset and I just wanted to reach out and hold you close. I know it sounds silly, but after we spoke in the car park last night I haven't been able to concentrate on anything else but you and how much fun we have together. The way you touch me. The way you laugh. Your big puppy dog eyes."

I couldn't help but find that interesting thing on the floor myself now as I felt my cheeks flush a little. I also couldn't help a little smile creeping onto my face, as the voice in my head began to scream at me *"Be strong!"* Will continued,

69

"I've never really had a girlfriend before, let alone a boyfriend and I think I just got scared when you said you loved me because I'm not sure that I love you." A shot of panic crossed his face before he quickly added "I don't mean that in a bad way."

I sat in silence as he continued,

"To be honest maybe I do, I've no idea. It's a whole new world of feelings going on for me right now and I'm also worried that you're not exactly coming from a stable position. It's really not long since you split up with your girlfriend. I could just be a rebound thing for you".

Now, there was a statement. All I'd done is think about the same thing for the last few months. I broke my silence,

"You're right to be cautious; I don't know what I'm doing at the moment." As I spoke, the clouds finally lifted and I knew I was being honest with myself as well as with Will.

"The only thing I know is that I was enjoying spending time with you and it felt right. Whether I end up with a girl or a guy next I really couldn't say."

"It must be really hard for you being your first relationship and I really wasn't trying to pressure you to declare your undying love for me." I giggled

"Gary." He was on his feet now and kneeling in front of me. I was holding my - breath what the hell was he doing?

"I'm sorry, can you forgive me?" he said looking me in the eye. I could see his pain and his yearning but couldn't help burst out laughing.

"I thought you were going to propose there for a second".

He looked down at the way he was on one knee and holding my hand and said,

"Well if you hadn't interrupted. But now you've ruined the

surprise I'll keep that for another time," and laughed. The ice was broken.

I suddenly felt a moment of real contentment and didn't care about the future, just what was happening there and then.

"Come here" I said and gave him a big hug and felt a surge of warmth run through my body. We held each other like that for a minute or so, not saying a word. I told him to go back to the sofa and joined him there hugging my knees and sipping my tea, properly ready to listen to him this time.

Will became quite animated as he explained more of his feelings. I think talking about his emotions was a completely new thing to him. I too, wanted to explain about my 'I love you' faux pas.

"I think I was just high in that post orgasmic state and I felt genuinely happy. More so than I have done in months and I think that's why I said what I said. I'll take it back if it makes you feel happier?"

"No! Don't take it back" he said a bit too quickly. Then he moved in to kiss me. It was a kiss that was so passionate and full of love, yet so soft, gentle and slow that it seemed to go on for about 10 minutes. I was tingly in all the right places and without another word, lead him up to my bedroom where we properly made up. It was intense but incredibly intimate and we lost ourselves in each other.

I lay in a dozy haze with Will in my arms neither of us saying a word but exchanging glances that said it all. I kissed him and then we both drifted off into our own lazy thoughts and then a glorious deep sleep took over.

We were awoken by Amanda coming up the stairs and calling my name.

"Gary! Oh Gazza? You up there?"

Shit! I didn't want her to see Will with me. Last she knew he was a heartbreaker and we'd split up. I felt like a teenager who was about to get caught out by my mum.

"Knock knock, wake up sleepy head or you'll not sleep tonight," she said and walked in. She saw Will and before I had the chance to say anything went beetroot,

"Sorry" she muttered.

Amanda closed the door and ran full speed down the stairs.

"Oh no," I said.

"What's wrong? She knows about us doesn't she?" said Will putting his arm around me.

"Well she does but she thinks you're a bastard who broke my heart." Will looked hurt.

"Oh I see."

"There's more" I added.

"I think she was kind of hoping that me and her would get together now that Ruth was out of the way."

"Oh no" said Will.

"Yep, that's what I said. We'd best get up and dressed," I said.

"Yeah, and I think it'd be best if I just headed off home," said Will as he pulled his boxer shorts on. I pulled him back to the bed and gave him a lingering kiss and let a bit of my insecurity show through

"We're ok then? Back on?"

"Most definitely," he said and planted another kiss on me,

"And you'll talk to me about you concerns first next time rather than making decisions on your own?" I questioned.

"Yes... I... will." He said each word followed by a kiss. I was getting aroused again.

"Oh thanks, Will. I can't go downstairs like this!" He just laughed and showed that he was in the same state. We restrained ourselves and ended up talking about the work meeting which soon cooled us down and we went downstairs to an awkward atmosphere with Amanda watching Coronation Street. As Will made his excuses I thought I was in for a grilling. Instead I got the silent treatment.

"Hey Amanda. How was your day?" I said upbeat.

"Ok," she said without taking her eyes of the TV. Silence followed and then one word answers as I asked her irritating questions about who was sleeping with whom in Corrie.

I was in the dog house that was for sure. It had been an emotional rollercoaster of a day, but Amanda didn't deserve how I'd treated her. My offer to make her tea was rebuffed and even though she was trying to smile as she said 'No', it was written all over her face at how angry she was.

The frosty atmosphere led me to make my excuses and retire to bed early. Despite my tiredness, sleep wouldn't take me. I'd slept with Will again. What was I doing? I couldn't even trust my own thoughts and feelings. I was a mess and Amanda knew this too. That's why she was cold with me – we both knew I shouldn't be with anyone, that I should just give myself time to be alone.

Next morning Amanda was up and out before me, which I was thankful for as I didn't want to see her. I was happy today, or at least telling myself I was. Will and I were back on and after the shame, hurt, tears and failed sexual advances I was ready to start a fresh. I arrived at work with a renewed vigour which was only boosted by Will's cheeky grin and sly gropes of my leg under the desk. I liked being naughty and this was very risky which only intensified the fun. The odd pat on the bum or breathing on each other's necks as we bumped into each other around the office made for a fun day but left me horny as hell so I arranged to go back to Will's place for dinner and plenty of afters.

When I got back home at about 11pm Amanda was waiting up like my mother; the mother I had been avoiding.

"I've been waiting for you. We need to talk." She said. I didn't like the sound of this, I'd had a good day and a fantastic evening and now she was set to ruin it.

"What's up?" I said light-heartedly.

"Please don't take this the wrong way, but I think it's time you moved out." Her words hung in the air not quite registering with me. She went on,

"We always knew that it was just for a little while until you got yourself sorted and to be honest I feel like I need my own space back." I was taken aback.

"Ok. Sure. Yes it was only temporary, you're right. I'll get on to the estate agents in the morning." I blurted out in shock.

"No rush. But you need to start looking" she said cheerily, the weight visibly lifting from her shoulders. I realised she must've been waiting all night for me to come home so she could say this.

"You're right and I really appreciate you letting me stay here as long as you have." I was sounding very business-like as I tried to stop the shock showing on my face.

"It's about time I left you in peace. You're probably sick of the sight of me." I was looking for reassurance, but I wasn't going to get any.

"Night then" she said as she went to bed.

I sat down on the sofa a little bit stunned. If only she hadn't walked in on Will and I yesterday and I could've broken the news more gently. I'm sure she'd have relaxed about it all and things could have gotten back to normal, whatever that was.

No, this wasn't about finding Will, it was to do with me and her wasn't it. I'd broken her heart and was now rubbing salt in the wounds. She's the one person I didn't want to hurt and it seemed that recently that's all I was doing. This arrangement was only ever supposed to be temporary and I had stayed longer than I ever intended. It was easy, and more than that, we were having a great time together and it allowed me to forget about Ruth and the whole gay thing. I resolved to make a real effort in the morning to find a new place; once I moved out our friendship would get back on track.

The next day I stayed true to my word and within a month I'd found a place. Amanda and I didn't really see much of each other in that month with her supposedly working late and me seeing a lot of Will. I think we'd both been purposely avoiding each other. This was the start of our friendship deteriorating; something I would never have thought possible.

Chapter 11

Will and I enjoyed the irony in our romance. He was a salesman and I was in the marketing department; never the twain shall be bedfellows was the feeling in the office. The sales department blamed the marketing department for all their problems and vice versa. If our colleagues ever found out about us we'd be the biggest scandal since the couple who snuck in at the weekend to have sex on their boss' desk on two separate occasions. (despite being caught and cautioned the first time!)

Automotive was a very male, testosterone fuelled industry and unsurprisingly there was no one in the office who was gay or even appeared to be so. To find out that two of the department were not only gay but sleeping together would blow everyone's minds.

Will was far from your typical salesman. He was one of the friendliest people in the office and took time to ask how you were getting on, in complete contrast to most of the pushy salesmen. I liked him from the first moment we met and we had a laugh together. He seemed really kind, gentle and laid back. Handsome, in a clean-cut way, with short, slightly curly, mousey brown hair and gorgeous aqua marine coloured eyes. He was slightly shorter than my five foot eleven and more stocky than my slim frame and always looked well presented in his suit and tie.

Our first real conversation was when someone up on high had the ingenious idea to bring the sales and marketing teams closer with a buddy system. Will and I were paired up and all set to go and visit one of Will's customers. I hadn't been at the company long at all and it was nice to have someone who felt welcoming and took time to explain things. This was about 18 months before that revealing night at the bowling alley.

Will and I chatted in the car on the way to the customer and got to know each other a bit better but never was there any inkling that Will was gay. Not that I was looking for it. He talked of his friends and appeared to have lots of male friends which met my expectations of a salesman. Will, however, gave nothing away about a girlfriend (or a boyfriend even).

Looking back on that first day now, it's quite ironic because we joked about one of the staff at the auto repair shop being very friendly to me and that he must fancy me. Little did I know that at the time Will was going through a tough time accepting that he was gay.

Will and I definitely bonded on that day but only the sort of friendship where you see each other in work and on nights out with other colleagues. It soon became apparent that we both had a touch of the Social Secretary about us and we started arranging nights out with a crowd from work. We were the younger ones and were more than up for going out and getting drunk. It wasn't until I'd split with Ruth though that he seemed to talk to me more on nights out.

Now that we were dating, albeit in secret from everyone else, I was really getting to know and like him even more. I also had the chance to talk to him more about how he'd known he was gay.

One night after work, I'd gone to his flat for dinner and we sat in a post-dinner stupor, snuggled up on the sofa in the living room of his two bedroom flat. He'd bought it six months ago as his first step on the property ladder. It wasn't the prettiest block of flats from the outside but it was really spacious inside and I guess the inside is the bit you see most of the time. The décor was a mish mash of furniture and fittings, as most first homes are; a new IKEA TV unit, a mahogany second hand sideboard and borrowed floral curtains. There was a pile of Playstation games including Crash Bandicoot and the latest WWE wrestling game beside the TV and as we sat on the floor locked in battle, I decided to ask Will more about being gay.

"Will. How long have you known you were gay?"

"Hmm it's hard to say. I've never really fancied girls and looking back I can think of times I felt something for the boys I used to play with when I was 5 or 6 years old. Obviously at that age I didn't recognise what that feeling was but by the time I was in my teens I think I knew but I tried to convince myself I was wrong." Said Will.

"So was coming out to Jane and I the first time you allowed yourself to believe it?" I asked.

"Not as such. I actually tried to come out to my mum a couple of years ago and, well, the look of horror on her face and her telling me it was probably just a phase, sent me back to hiding it. Mum knows best and all that."

Will was smiling but I could tell he was hurt thinking back at his mum's reaction.

"Was this around the time you tried to get with that girl?" I asked.

"Yeah. In a last ditch do-or-die approach, I decided to go

and stay with Sophie when she was studying in Cambridge." Will said.

"My intention was to go there and lose my virginity, proving that I was straight and this whole gay thing was, like Mum had said, just a phase." Will laughed,

"As we both know it didn't work."

I can't really imagine the emotions he was feeling on the trip up to Cambridge. I myself had lost my virginity at 17 to Ruth and would've lost it much earlier given the chance. How he had managed to keep himself chaste for 25 years of his life is beyond me; he didn't appear to have badly blistered palms.

Will went on to describe the feelings he had at the time as ones of stoic determination – he would plough that furrow, ravage that woman and make the world an easier place all round. However, when it came to it he just couldn't rise to the occasion, not that it got anywhere near the stage that he'd have needed to. His conscience kicked in and left him having to come out to a girl that was clearly thinking she'd found Mr Right. In many ways a similar situation to Amanda and I, but at the same time completely different. This was a neighbour he'd grown up with: a very sweet girl by the name of Sophie who had always had a sparkle in her eye for Will, not that he ever noticed.

She had hit Will with a tirade of questions including *'How do you know, if you've never been with a woman?'* An interesting question. One that would land you a punch should you ever dare twist it and ask a straight man how he knew he wasn't gay if he'd never slept with a man. I guess the instinct from Sophie was to make him realise he was straight so she'd have her Prince Charming back and stop her ego from being dented at the fact that she couldn't make a man want to have sex with her.

"I suggested it would be best if I just drove on home that night rather than spend the weekend. Sophie seemed a little disappointed as if she thought *'Give me the weekend and I'll turn you.'* and persuaded me to stay. We talked it out over the weekend and although awkward she was great with me." Will finished his Sophie story and went to put the kettle on. I sat deep in thought.

At work I'd heard several of the girls talking about him and he was considered quite the eligible bachelor, but no woman ever really pursued him heavily enough to warrant him being put in a position of awkwardness. To his university and school friends, who were all straight men, he was just Will and his lack of luck with the ladies only gave them more ammunition to tease him. As you'd expect there's only so long you can keep denying something, and now, Will had reached his threshold. Jane and I were amongst the first round of 'comings out' that Will had done. In fact we were fourth and fifth in line after his mum, Sophie and someone else from work. Actually we'd be more like sixth and seventh as he told his mum (again) and dad after telling the other guy from work. Neither his mum nor his dad, seemed to want to acknowledge what Will was saying. Perhaps they just didn't know what to say. They just kept on with whatever they were doing and pretended that Will had just told them something completely insignificant: *'That's nice dear. Could you hand me that trowel please.'*

What should a parent say? When you're going through coming out you can only think of your own hardship and you don't really think how it will affect those you love because all you care about is being accepted by those same people. To hear them say it doesn't change anything and to give you a big hug is all you want. When you get a lukewarm or even a bad reaction it is heart breaking and maddening at the same time.

I thought about Will's parents and how maybe they would be in shock, or even disappointed that their child was different. Maybe they would be worried or feel overprotective about what being gay means for his life and future. Perhaps they would start wondering if it was their DNA or the way they had raised him that made him gay. Hell, maybe they are blaming each other; if she hadn't been so doting or soft on him, if he had played more sports with him etc. Probably they would just need time to process it all in their heads.

As Will returned with a cup of tea, he wore a big grin,

"What's making you laugh?" I asked.

"Well, when I came out to Mum and Dad again recently, my mate Dan really put his foot in it." Started Will.

"Dan was round at the flat as we were meeting some other friends up in London and he was getting ready here. I was in the shower when the phone went so Dan picked it up. It was my mum and Dan has always had a jokey relationship with her and for some reason thought it would be funny to say *'He's upstairs with his boyfriend.'* Which couldn't have been worse timing, considering I'd only come out to her again the day before."

I burst out laughing and soon we were both laughing our heads off. I think there was something of an exaggerated laugh for Will as he released some pent up tension from the event.

"That is brilliantly bad. I bet you were panicked about what your mum was thinking." I said.

"I bloody was! I couldn't get it out of my head all night and wasn't able to ring her either as Dan and the others would've heard the conversation." Will replied.

"I had to go round there next day and have a very awkward conversation explaining that Dan doesn't know and I didn't have some secret boyfriend that I was hiding from her." Will paused.

"But I guess I do now?"

"Boyfriend? You should be so lucky. You're just a hot piece of rebound ass for me." I teased.

"I'm being serious Gary. I want you to meet my parents." Said Will.

"Okay." I agreed. I painted on a smile but felt the fear well up inside me. Will looked excited as he told me he would suggest going to them this Sunday for lunch.

* * *

As Sunday arrived, I was absolutely shitting myself. The last time I had to meet my partner's parents I was 16 and it seems much less of a big deal at that age as you're invincible, or so it feels. Plus this time I had the added pressure of possibly being a partner the parents would never approve of due to the fact I was a guy.

I must've tried about three different shirts on and was starting to lose it with Will who kept giving the same *"You look fine"* answer. Fine? Fine? I didn't want to look fine, I wanted to look perfect.

I'd met his mother once before on that first day that Will and I had gone out on a work trip as he was still living at home at the time. I'd agreed to meet him there first thing and we'd share a car to the auto repair shops we were visiting. I remembered her as a smiley woman, quite timid, but welcoming enough. That was then and this was now. We were in the car and on the way to their house for Sunday lunch and I wasn't feeling remotely hungry as my stomach flipped. I kept fidgeting and checking my hair in the visor mirror.

"What if they don't like me? What should I talk about? How long do we have to stay?" I rambled, not even giving Will a chance to respond.

"Shh, shhh calm down. You'll be fine. You look gorgeous and I'm the one you need to worry about impressing. You're my boyfriend, not theirs. Besides, what's not to love about you? Everyone loves Gary," said Will comfortingly. My silence must've made him think his calming words had succeeded and they did for a second or two, but then came the panic again.

"Aren't you even the slightest bit nervous?" I shrieked a little too loudly.

"You need to calm down." Will said gently.

"Of course I'm nervous, but excited too. I'm looking forward to showing you off. They'll love you. Trust me." I decided to spend the rest of the journey just taking long, slow, deep breaths.

The car pulled up outside. We'd arrived. I got out of the car and followed Will nervously into the house and was nearly bowled over by his parent's massive dog, Flash, who was actually giving me a very warm welcome. I just hoped it wasn't going to be a damp one too.

"Get out of it!" shouted Will's dad and I was about to turn and leave in shock when Will grabbed my arm and whispered,

"He's talking to the dog."

Will's mum supressed a laugh at that point and I had hopes that things would turn out alright after all. We walked into the lounge and I shook Will's dad's hand.

"Geoff. Pleased to meet you." He said. "This is my wife

Eileen."

I wasn't sure of the etiquette so ended up doing an awkward hug into handshake, air kiss thing. I really was very nervous.

Coats were taken and tea offers accepted as we sat down to make small talk. For some reason I felt that I had to butch things up with Geoff. He was a man's man and quite old fashioned, I'm pretty sure he wouldn't want his son to be dating a camp guy.

After the usual pleasantries about the weather and how lovely their home was we moved to the dining table to have a freshly made roast dinner.

I can't say the conversation was natural and free flowing, but it was polite and I got through it. I think they liked the opportunity to talk about the things they were passionate about (upholstery for her and golf for him). The worst part was probably when Will was in the kitchen with his mum and I was left with his dad trying to converse on football with my incredibly limited knowledge. Why I just didn't say *I'm not into football* I'll never know.

Out of the corner of my eye I could see Will and Eileen giggling and chatting to each other and his mum seemed to be nodding and they both glimpsed my way and when they saw me looking they burst out laughing. Geoff could feel my embarrassment so decided to call over Flash and make him roll over and give his paw. Something, I would later discover, he does whenever anyone new comes to the house. Then Will came back in to the room with a massive beam on his face and gave me a 'thumbs up' behind his dad's back – I was a hit with his mum at least.

* * *

With his parents introduced and on board with our relationship, Will's confidence in coming out was riding high. We'd been seeing each other for about six months now and he decided it was time to start telling his friends. I could tell he was apprehensive about telling his best friends though. I think Will was worried that they might start to look back at times in the past where they'd wrestled as teenagers or even showered at the gym and feel like Will had somehow been getting a thrill out of it. I was most worried about his best friends Dan and Mark.

Will decided it would be best to tell them at the same time, so arranged a night out of drinking. The guys were having a laugh taking the mickey out of each other and talking about nothing in particular. Will was beginning to get cold feet and considered not telling them but after a pep talk in the pub toilet mirror, he came back and immediately said,

"Guys, I've got something to tell you. There's no easy way to say it so I'll just come out with it – I'm gay." There was a long pause before Mark started laughing.

"Aaah! You nearly had us then! Good one". Said Dan.

"Wanker!" joined Mark and laughed. Will was not laughing and suddenly the other two realised that he wasn't joking.

"You're not serious are you?" questioned Dan disdainfully.

"Yep, I'm afraid I am," said Will, expecting the guys to ask the usual questions about how did he know etc. Instead he got Dan looking aghast and Mark heading for the bar. Will tried to talk to Dan but he was in shock and didn't seem to want to talk about it.

"What you do behind closed doors is your business. You don't have to share it with us though. I just don't want to know." He said. Will was gobsmacked, this was one of his best friends making him feel like he was some sort of sexual deviant who should keep his filthy, secret perversions behind closed doors and hidden away with the shame they deserved. Will was lost for words – this had not gone to plan. Mark returned with two pints and a Babycham giving the latter to Will,

"Thought this'd be more your style now." he said in a jokey way, but one that was laced with a certain venom. Will wasn't having it.

"Cheers guys. Nice to know you can count on your friends in difficult times. Stick your Babycham up your arse Mark and fuck you very much Dan!" He said. It was completely out of character for Will and he stormed out of the bar.

Will returned to me that night and I struggled to keep a straight face when he recounted his parting shot. He was furious as he brought me up to speed with Dan and Mark's reaction. It was odd to hear Will swear or see him get angry, he was usually so calm and placid. I wasn't expecting him that night, so I knew things hadn't gone well when he turned up on my doorstep just before 10.00 p.m.

As I've mentioned Will isn't the type to get emotional, but tonight after a few drinks and the bad reaction of two of his closest friends, he was close to tears. He was fluctuating between anger and worry that he might've lost his pals. I was very much a coming out novice, having only told Will and Amanda, and I told him he'd done the right thing, pulling out the cliché; '*Screw your friends if they can't deal with it, they're not worth having as friends*'. Why is it always so easy to dish out advice and make it sound so easy when it's not you that has to heed it? My mind was starting to whir and think of how I'd tell my friends, and how they'd react; would I lose any through coming out?

I managed to calm Will down a little, but he wanted to go to bed and I got the feeling he wanted to be left alone so I stuck on The Assassin DVD and tried not to worry about the little things. By the time I snuck into the bed beside him, Will was fast asleep. I was beginning to realise that Will could fall asleep in minutes in pretty much any situation.

Next morning Will was feeling a bit stronger about it all and willing to stand his ground. However, he also wanted to talk to Dan and Mark again because it could've just been the initial shock. We had another customer visit that day so got in the car together and off we went. Will put his phone on hands free and realising he had a message played it. It was Mark.

"Hey Will, how's your arse this morning? Did you pick up some bender on the way home to bum? Thanks for the drink although I think the Babycham may have pushed me over the edge. Speak to you soon Gaylord".

He was clearly drunk and showing off to Dan, but what an idiot. Will went very quiet and I could see he was seething. The strange thing with Dan and Mark is that I'd already met them once or twice on nights out and I thought Mark was a bit odd then. He seemed to be proving me right. Now that Will and I were together I was very protective and started to rant only to be told to shut up by Will. I took the hint. He wanted to deal with this in his own way.

We continued the journey in silence, only to be interrupted by a phone call from Mark. We could both see his name on the caller ID screen and I was curious to see if Will would answer as I'd be able to hear every word of the conversation. The ringing continued and Will let it slip through to answerphone.

"Please don't say a word." Will said as he sensed my preparatory in-breath. *Beep beep. Beep beep.* Mark had left a message. I was desperate to play it but pretended to be deep in thought looking out the window instead. I could feel Will's desire to play the message too, but in loyalty to his friend, he wanted to screen the message first. About five minutes went by and then he caved in and played the message.

"Hi Will….it's Mark" said a very sheepish voice.

"I'm sorry about the message I left you last night. I was just messing with you. You know what I'm like after a few drinks." He sounded sincere and guilty to boot, as he continued,

"Anyway give me a call. Oh and don't worry about Dan he'll come around."

Well at least Mark had apologised and seemingly accepted Will, that is, until the next time he was drunk, I suspected. But what did he mean about Dan? I couldn't bite my lip any longer.

"How do you feel about that?" I asked Will. He wasn't happy and I knew it was about Dan.

"Well that's just typical Mark isn't it. He's a nightmare when he's drunk. Bit concerned about Dan though. The two of them have obviously been talking and Dan looked visibly stunned when I told him. He's clearly not taken it well." Will replied.

"I'll have to give him a call." I couldn't really understand why Will was being so protective of his friends. I'd have made them suffer for being such arses, but Will wanted to handle things in his own way.

Dan managed to avoid all Will's calls in the first week following the revelation and Will was getting increasingly frustrated and worried. I suggested he phone Mark and get him to arrange a meet up for them all. Mark and Will had already met up again and gone through all Mark's questions and to my surprise, there were no more drunken phone messages. Mark managed to get Dan, although reluctantly, to agree to meet with Will.

The whole night through he could barely look Will in the eye, the conversation was stilted and every time Will tried to make a joke about being gay, or remind Dan of the phone call with his mum, Dan just changed the subject. By the end of the night, Will could take no more.

"Look Dan, we've got to talk about it. I'm gay and you will just have to deal with it." Dan looked Will in the eye for the first time that night,

"It's not right Will" he said abruptly, then softened.

"Maybe you've just not met the right girl yet?" Will shook his head and sighed.

"I've been trying to find the right girl for years…. and it turns out her name is Gary." Dan looked puzzled

"What, the Gary from your work that we've been out drinking with?" Will nodded.

"Jeez you're all over the place aren't you? I thought he had a girlfriend?"

"He did but that was over long ago and now we're together." Will replied. Dan screwed up his face and Will let out a frustrated sigh, looking for the right words.

"Look Dan. I didn't choose to be gay. It's just the way I am. I'm not suddenly going to start wearing crop tops and mincing around. I'm the same person you've always known, but I'm happier than ever." He then muttered,

"I'm in love. Be happy for me, Dan, and don't worry - I'm not going to try and bum you every time I see you. I might be gay but I'm not blind or desperate." Will tried to lighten

89

the mood and Dan nearly cracked a smile, easing the tension momentarily before he slipped back to serious mode.

"I'm sorry mate, but I just don't get it. Maybe it's because you've been living on your own. You could go and see a shrink?" He said. Will, couldn't believe what he was hearing, but knew that Dan wasn't trying to be caustic.

"Thanks for your advice Trisha but I don't need to see a shrink. I'm gay and I'm pretty sure that I was born that way so you're just going to have to deal with it." Adding some emotional blackmail,

"You're one of my best friends and I need you to be there for me." Dan shifted uncomfortably in his seat.

"I just don't know any gay people. I'm being honest with you. I'm struggling with this so please just give me time." Will and Dan agreed to take things slowly with all things gay.

* * *

We decided not to force our coupledom down their throats, but Will did want us to go out with both Mark and Dan so arranged a group night out. After some initial awkwardness, we all relaxed into what was more like a group of lads out on the lash. Everything seemed to have gone well and Will was beaming as we got the train home and he sat next to me, secretly stroking my hand.

Next day, we were both in good spirits and decided to go for a walk in the park to clear our fuzzy heads. It was a short car journey to the park and as we got in the car Will plugged in his mobile as was his habit. *Beep beep, Beep beep* - there was a voice message.

Will pressed the correct series of buttons as we sat there awaiting the message to play through the car stereo speakers.

"Hey Will it's Mark.."

That's as far as Will let it play before hitting disconnect.

"I think I'll listen to that a little later…just in case" Will laughed.

Chapter 12

Will had done the deed and told all his friends and family about us. We were living in our happy little world, but I still hadn't told any of my family and only one of my friends – it was still my dirty little secret.

I'm sure I was just putting it off, but the reality was that on a day-to-day basis it didn't affect my family and a lot of my friends who didn't live in the area. That said, I really needed to start to tell people and why shouldn't I shout about it; I was happy again.

I thought I'd start with Jane as she had responded really well to Will coming out to us that night at the bowling alley. Surely she'd be just as understanding of me coming out?

I arranged to meet her in our local pub, as we often did, for a drink after work. I arrived first, got a bottle of wine in and found a table purposely away from the busy bar area. I was surprisingly nervous, despite Will reassuring me earlier in the day. In fact, he'd offered to come along too but I felt I owed it to Jane to tell her on my own.

My nerves calmed when Jane greeted me with a warm smile and even warmer hug. We started talking straight away and it must have been at least an hour into our conversation that Jane brought up Amanda. The pair had met through various get togethers I'd held and hit it off straight away. We'd all been out for drinks the week before with Will and some other friends from the office.

"Am I being paranoid or was Amanda a bit off with you when we went to Scruffy Murphys last Friday?" said Jane.

"Is everything alright between the two of you?"

"Well not exactly. That's kind of why I wanted to have this drink with you tonight." I said.

"You want me to act as go-between? I'm not sure I'm comfortable doing that as I don't really know her that well and I don't want to get stuck in the middle." She quickly got in.

"No it's not that." I said.

"It's more to do with why she's unhappy with me." I took a sip of drink as Jane leaned in.

"You know what Will told us at the bowling alley just over a year ago?" Jane nodded.

"Well I think the same applies to me." I said and looked at the table top as I finished with "In fact, Will and I are seeing each other."

There was silence as she ordered her thoughts in her head so she didn't say the wrong thing.

"Are you sure?" she said. "It's really not been long since you split from Ruth. You sure that you're really gay?"

She was having trouble comprehending.

"I'm as certain as I can be. I don't know if I'm gay or bi-sexual, but right now I'm falling in love with Will," I said.

"I'm happy. So be happy for me please. I couldn't stand to lose you too," I said and touched her forearm.

"Don't be silly. You're stuck with me. I just don't want to see you get hurt again. Will and you are both in very delicate places. It's all fresh and new to both of you and I just want to be confident that you're sure."

I was touched by her concern. What she was saying was hitting a nerve, but all I had was hope in my heart. Hope that Will and I would work out.

"I'm sure," I said, then filled her in on the Amanda situation, the failed seduction and the strained friendship.

"Don't give up on Amanda. To be fair I always did get the feeling she was carrying a candle for you. Give her some space and time and hopefully you two will be thick as thieves again in no time." Jane said.

* * *

That was Jane and Amanda told and of course all Will's friends that he'd outed me to. It was much easier to be introduced as Will's boyfriend as I didn't have to say the words *I'm gay*. I still choked up though and looked ashamed as I shook Will's friends' hands. Why did I have it in me that being gay is such a bad thing to be or somehow made me less of a man? It can have only come from my upbringing and the environment I grew up in.

Will and I had been together for almost a year now, still in secret to most people at work, my family and most of my friends. Will had decided to sell his flat and buy a new place, but so far had been unlucky in that the places he kept trying to buy kept falling through. He had a buyer lined up for his flat and couldn't keep them hanging on any longer so decided to move back into his parents' house. I had other ideas.

"You could move in to my flat?" I said hopefully, continuing with,

"You're here virtually every night anyway."

There was a nervous anticipation and Will looked like he did that day he dumped me. My heart was thumping. I'd done it again hadn't I? We'd been revelling in those first stages of a new relationship: wanting to spend every minute together, learning about and introducing each other to new things: WWE, South Park and Kylie mainly. I was about to rescind the line or try to play it off as a joke but Will interrupted.

Looking at the floor he said,

"I really don't think that I …" I didn't like where this was going, "…can say no!"

He beamed and then hugged me; he was winding me up and he nearly got me too. I gave him a quick punch in the arm as the tension evaporated.

I drifted off into my own thoughts as he held me. Here I was 18 months on from splitting up with Ruth, now I was moving my boyfriend in with me. I never saw that one coming. It was a joyous feeling but also one that reminded me that I still hadn't told my family.

I'd told Amanda and it had estranged us, making me anxious about telling other friends. Ever since she found Will in bed with me things hadn't been the same. She was deliberately putting space between us and was doing the things that we used to do together with other friends, as if to spite me. I wasn't taking it too well, but at the same time I had Will and was still enjoying spending time with him and of course was meeting all his friends so my social circle had doubled. I was in love and I couldn't understand why Amanda wasn't happy for me.

Aside from Amanda, my life was looking up. Will had agreed to move in and I was about to start my new job in the TV industry. After about eight months of rejections from trying all the TV production houses and channels, I'd gotten lucky after seeing an ad in Broadcast (a TV industry trade magazine) and applying. Two interviews later I had landed myself a new job. I had my first contract as a Researcher for a new reality show called 'Some Mothers Do Push Em'. It was all about pushy parents and their talented brats. The talents ranged from cringe-worthy singing and dancing through to juggling and some more unusual skills.

It's always quite nervous starting a new job as well as exciting, of course, and I had to keep pinching myself – me, working in TV.

On my first day I was paired up with Ebonee who already had three projects under her belt despite being a year younger than me. She had studied TV and Film at Liverpool John Moores University and her greeting was friendly and extremely confident. Also on the team was Shaun who was 18 and a runner (basically everyone's lackey) and he was camp as Christmas. Really out and proud; it scared me. How could someone so young have no fear? Ultimately I was envious of his outness and ability to be comfortable with who he was.

I was 24 and had been gay for about a year. I tried to reconcile that statement I'd just made in my own mind, gay for about a year; wasn't I always gay? I couldn't face that minefield right now. For now I was just nervous that Shaun would clock me and tell everyone I was gay and then they'd all judge me. I could feel my head looking down as I shook Shaun's hand in an overly firm way to emphasise my manliness. This only made things worse as he retorted with a excited camp comment,

"Oooh what a tight grip you have!"

I wanted the floor to open up and swallow me whole. Everyone laughed and I quickly manoeuvred my position to say hello to the next team member, Jake.

He was the Senior Researcher and was a real cockney playboy type. I felt scared of him in another way but drew on all the laddish behaviour I'd learnt from my brothers to make small talk with him.

At the top was the director; a 50 year old man named Henry. Incredibly well spoken and dressed in cords and a striped pink shirt complete with a coordinating cravat. He was old school – TV and money. His handshake lingered a little too long as did his gaze when I introduced myself. He was clearly trying to bore into my soul and figure out what sort of person I was, and something else…surely he wasn't coming on to me?

To my surprise the producer came along at the same time and Henry introduced me to Penny - his wife. I guess my Gaydar wasn't that good after all. Maybe Shaun was straight too?

I would later discover that sexual ambiguity is a regular occurrence in the Entertainment industry – you just never can be sure which way someone swings unless you ask…or catch them in the act.

They were a friendly enough crew and I soon eased up on my nerves and was producing some good work. I even managed to find a child whose talent was to be a human table. She'd literally do a crab and the mother would place a lightweight Perspex sheet on her stomach to create a table. It was one of the most bizarre things I've ever seen but the mother encouraged the child to do this. They had become quite the spectacle at the local shopping mall where she'd take two chairs and they'd pour tea and eat cake with her daughter literally bending over backwards to accommodate as the portable table she was. Henry thought it made a great story and break from all the pageant style singers.

The very nature of the TV world is that your work is very much project based and once a show is done, you move on to another with a completely new team. I think that because of this it was easier for me to fit in as everyone was like the new boy to an extent. I think it was the third day that Ebonee asked me if I had a girlfriend in front of Shaun and Jake. I panicked and had said yes before I knew it.

"Her name? Wils, short for Wilma. She hates her name because of the Flintstones." I said, embellishing my lie. After that though, it was easy to just tell the truth about how we met and what she did because she was obviously Will. However, I felt bad for lying to them, especially Ebonee who I was warming up to as the weeks went on. Plus I had to keep making excuses as to why I didn't bring Wils out to meet them on our weekly Friday team drinks. They were all gagging to meet this wonderful lady.

Now that I'd lied it would be a really big thing to come clean, but I felt like I owed it to Ebonee in particular. I suggested the two of us grab some lunch. We commandeered a table in the canteen and sat down.

"Ebs, I've got something to tell you," I said.

"What's up Gary?" she asked concerned.

"It's about Wils." My heart was pounding and my throat went dry. I don't know if it was the truth or the fact that I'd lied that was worrying me more.

"She's not exactly, well a girl." There was silence and I continued "I don't have a girlfriend, I have a boyfriend called Will."

To my surprise Ebonee let out a big breath and started to laugh.

"I thought you were going to say she was a dog or something. Thankfully she is just a he."

"Yeah. Sorry to have lied to you, but even though we've been together for over a year I've not really told many people that I'm gay." The last bit was whispered.

"It's okay." she whispered back and looked around in a conspiring way,

"I hear there's quite a few of them in these parts. Your secret's safe with me." She laughed again.

"To be honest it has never crossed my mind. Does this mean we'll finally get to meet Wils." She said, using her fingers to make air speech marks around Wils

"And will he wear a dress anyway?"

"I don't think so. Not with his hips." I joked back.

"I'd actually really like you to meet him. But I guess that means I'll have to tell the others too." I said.

"Actually one of the team thought you were gay from day one," she said with a raised eyebrow.

"Who?" I said intrigued and a bit offended at the same time. There it was again, that feeling that it's somehow an insult to be gay.

"Shaun no doubt?" I said.

"Nope" she said, "Guess again."

"Not Jake?" I suggested.

"Nope. Time is running out Gazza. You have one guess left." Ebonee was enjoying this a bit too much.

"Surely not Henry?" I said.

"Wak wak ooops. Oh! So close but incorrect. Let's see viewers who it was." She made a drumroll with her fingers on the table top - "Penny!"

"Really? Now that does surprise me. When did she say that?" I asked, surprised.

"After she met you on the first day she asked me and Shaun, and Shaun said no way. He'll need to fix his Gaydar." She laughed again.

"I think I need to check mine too because I thought Henry was gay when I first met him." I said.

Ebonee leaned in and did the checking-over-her-shoulders motion again as she whispered.

"Well he sort of is."

My eyes went wide.

"No!" I said a little too loudly, drawing attention from the other diners. I looked round, pretending I was looking for the source of the noise just like everyone else in the canteen. Ebonee was leaning in again.

"Apparently he swings both ways and they have an open relationship. Penny told me when she'd had a few too many drinks a couple of Fridays ago."

Ebonee loved to gossip and here she was spreading it again. I was hooked.

"Maybe my gaydar is fine then. When we met it was like he was sizing me up for dinner," I said.

"Wouldn't surprise me." She said stirring her Diet Coke with a straw. She was building up to something even more shocking; I recognised the signs. She would play with something and look disinterested as if to let you get comfortable and then she drops the bombshell, but only if you play along.

"He tried it on with both Shaun and Jake."

My jaw dropped.

"No!" I said, in a lower voice this time. She looked up from

100

her drink, beaming with *'ask me for more information'* all over her face. I think that's how she justified being a gossip – you had to make her tell you, which wasn't difficult at all you just had to ask the right questions.

"Jake? What did he think he was doing? Tell me that's not how Shaun got his job is it?" Ebonee opened her mouth to speak, but I quickly spoke over her when I noticed Shaun approaching our table.

"Hi Shaun. You want to join us?"

"I will sit down for 5 minutes but Henry wants me in his office. Some special job for me." He said. Ebonee couldn't help it; she spat out her drink and had to pretend it had gone down the wrong way.

"You alright Ebs? Having trouble swallowing?" I asked, which only set her off again. She managed to compose herself a little and replied,

"Sit down Shaun. Gary has something to tell you. I'm off to the laydeeez room."

Shaun pulled up a chair and sat down eagerly.

"Ooh what have you got to tell me?"

"Well...I...erm...haven't quite been telling the truth about my girlfriend." I slowly got out.

"What has she only got one leg or something?" said Shaun making himself laugh.

"It's well, that she isn't a 'she' at all but a 'he'" I said.

"O-M-G!" Shouted Shaun far too loudly, but rather than be embarrassed when everyone looked round he did something that would embarrass me far more.

"What?" he shouted.

"My friend here has just told me that he's one of us. Am I not allowed to be shocked? I mean come on, does his dress

101

sense say gay to you?"

I slumped down in my chair and put my hands over my face. Soon my little secret would be round the whole building. Shaun didn't even realise what he'd done. I think he was born gay and had always worn his gayness with pride. Why wasn't I so comfortable about it?

"Sooooo when do we meet this boyf of yours? How long have you been together? Is he hot? What does he look like? Got any pics? Has he got any nice friends? Lord knows I could do with a decent shag, I've not had one since a fortnight ago." Shaun drifted back to an action replay in his mind.

"Jan from Sweden. Shame he had to go home. He was a keeper. Still might be a cheap holiday eh? I'd only need to pay for the flight." He nudged me.

"So come on tell me all." He urged.

I spent the rest of the lunch hour not looking at anyone else in the canteen and being interrogated by Shaun and Ebonee. When we went back to the office word had indeed spread. Jake greeted me.

"Hey Gary, 'Wils' you give me a hand – not a job you dirty git." He said.

"You've heard then." I replied.

"Yep." said Jake.

"But why didn't you feel you could tell us? It's no big deal. Half the men here are gay." As he said this, those that were turned with pursed lips and shot us a dirty look.

As I went through the explanation with Jake, Henry walked past and winked at me. 'Oh no, here we go' I thought.

"Gary, can I see you in my office a minute please" he said. Ebonee put her tongue in her cheek and made a rude gesture.

"Just say No!" She started singing the old Grange Hill song.

I made my way very nervously to Henry's office where he stood by the door, ready to trap his victim – me! He was standing very close to me and his mouth was centimetres away from my ear.

"Please sit down." He said as he closed the door and walked round to take his seat on the other side of the desk.

"You know why I wanted to see you?" he questioned.

Because you've heard I'm gay and you want me to spend some time under your desk? I didn't think that was the smartest career move so instead I said,

"No. Something wrong?"

I was beginning to feel really hot and bothered.

"Nothing is wrong. Quite the contrary." He leaned over his desk a little.

"You know how much I like you Gary." He smiled. Oh no here it comes what do I say? Thanks, but no thanks? My career in TV was only just beginning and I needed to have a good recommendation from Henry to get other projects. Henry went on,

"Your work on this project has been phenomenal, but just between you and I, the show is not going to get commissioned. I found out this morning. However I have been given another project. It's another reality TV show trying to find the next star of the musicals. I can't say who, but a major name is on board as a judge, so I'm sure it's going to be massive."

Why was he telling me all this and when would he get to the open wide bit? I wanted to get the awkwardness of rejecting him out of the way. Henry took a deep breath and said,

"I want you Gary."

It hung in the air and the look on my face must've read as fear and non-comprehension because he went on to clarify.

"I want you to work on the show as one of the Senior Researchers."

It took a while for what he'd said to sink in and then the smile to grow on my face.

"Wow. I don't know what to say." I was lost for words; this isn't what I'd expected to happen at all. This was my first job in TV and here he was offering me a step up the ladder and on a show that sounded like it could be prime time viewing.

"Well say yes, dear boy." He egged me on.

"Of course. Yes! Thank you." I shook his hand and stood up to leave.

"Oh and Gary, please don't tell the rest of the crew any of what I've just told you. I don't want morale to slip. Tell them it was your probationary check-up or that I was making a pass at you." He laughed, and so did I in an over-the-top way. My head was still screaming 'Run, Gary Run!'

I left the room and gave the probation story to Ebonee, Shaun and Jake who crowded round me in a very unsubtle way. Ebonee confessed she'd actually been winding me up about Henry, had made it all up to tease me. I had to give her credit, she had me fooled.

What a day. I couldn't keep the smile off my face the whole way home. I'd come out to all my work colleagues and learnt a valuable lesson that it was much easier to just be upfront when asked a direct question about my romantic situation, rather than dig a hole I'd later have to climb out of.

Chapter 13

On this new roll of confidence, I decided it was time to tell my two best friends; one from school and one from university, both of whom were male. First up was Colin who lived on the south coast and had come up to see me for the weekend.

Colin is a very placid, genuinely nice guy. He's very private and doesn't really like talking about himself much, but is great company. We shared several classes at university and became firm friends, often going out clubbing and spending hours battling on Street Fighter and Tekken.

He arrived at lunchtime on Saturday and we went straight out to the Kings Arms nearby for a pint and burger. It was great to see him, although I knew that I was going to tell him my big news so was constantly looking for the right opportunity.

He had some big news of his own and was bursting to tell me, which was nice to see as usually he doesn't like to big himself up.

"I've got a new job." He said. I raised my near empty pint glass,

"Congratulations! What is it?" I said.

"I'm going to be working for a company that sells cruises." He said, beaming.

"Whatever floats your boat!" I chuckled at my own joke and saw that Colin was laughing along too.

"But seriously, that's great news. I think that deserves another pint. Same again?" I asked.

Colin picked up his remaining third of a pint and downed it in one, looking very pleased with himself before saying,

"Twist my arm then." We chatted for the rest of the afternoon getting just the right side of tipsy. Colin was on great form and I let him do much of the talking as he was clearly on a high. I dithered whether to tell him about Will and decided to leave it for now as we headed to the pool table.

It was about 11.30pm when we stumbled merrily into my flat. Will was away for the weekend so Colin was sleeping with me in the double bed because I only had a one bedroom flat and the sofa was too small. We'd done this many times at uni so it felt very normal. Maybe it wasn't my best idea to come out to him whilst in bed together, but in my drink addled mind, there was no time like the present.

"Colin," I said.

"Yes Gary." He replied.

"I've got to tell you something."

"Yes Gary?"

"I'm seeing someone."

He sat up on his elbow all excited.

"I knew it! It's Amanda isn't it?" he said triumphantly.

"Er no, it's not" I said. I was taken aback that yet another person seemed to have seen that Amanda fancied me when I'd completely missed it.

"Jane then. Must be Jane. I thought you seemed happier of late. How long have you been seeing her?" Asked Colin.

I didn't know how to tell him, but thought I'd just better

come out with it.

"It's not Jane either. It's Will."

He slunk back down deflated.

"Oh, right." He seemed to pull the covers tightly round his face and stare wide-eyed at the ceiling. I didn't like the silence so I explained to him how it had all come about and that it didn't change who I was etc. He was still very quiet but gave the odd 'mmm hmmm' and 'yeah' in the right places. I didn't think it had gone very well and cursed myself for telling him whilst we were in bed together.

"Night then" I said, thinking that he'd just want to go to sleep and get out of the bed as quickly as possible, but I was surprised that he started to open up after I'd turned the light off.

"A lot of people think that I'm gay you know. Because I've been single for quite a while." He started, and it was my turn to make the appropriate noises of encouragement.

"I'm not, in case you were wondering. I just haven't found any girls that I want to be with and the longer I leave it, the harder it gets." He sighed and I resisted the urge to make a smutty comment. He went on,

"It doesn't matter to me if you're gay. As long as you're happy, mate, that's good with me. Will seems like a nice guy from what I've seen of him so good luck to you." He turned away from me and I just about heard him say,

"If only I could find someone to be happy with."

I hated it when people had thought that I was gay when I was growing up, in fact I still didn't like people thinking I was gay now, even though I was. Plus I'd been from one relationship straight into another and he'd been single ever since we met at university. He wasn't the type to sleep around and I had probably wondered if he might be gay at some stage too. Not because he seemed gay in any way, but because it was unusual for someone to be single for so long. Now I knew for sure he wasn't, because this would've been the perfect time to come out if he was.

* * *

The next pal I had to tell would not be so easy. It was Ed; the guy who I shared my first gay sexual encounter with, no matter how technical it had been. We hadn't talked about it since. We had drifted when Ed went to university in Edinburgh and whenever we did see each other nothing was ever mentioned about what we'd done around the time of my 18th birthday. In fact, the subject was very taboo, with Ed changing topics if I even started talking about sex in general.

He had met a girl at university and been with her ever since. Her name was Louise and I have to say that I didn't instantly warm to her. Now I thought about it, it could've been jealousy of a kind or maybe it was just a pal looking out for his mate. I swear that hand on my heart I didn't fancy Ed, but ever since we did what we did all those years ago, there was definitely some weird connection between us; a kind of electricity or chemistry that surfaced from time to time.

Now a few years since we'd both left university I was on my way to have dinner with him and Louise. Ed had recently proposed to Louise and they'd invited me to have dinner with them to celebrate. I'd barely got in the door of their flat when Louise thrust her hand under my nose.

"Have you seen the ring? It's lovely isn't it?" she gushed.

"Yes. Very nice" I feigned interest.

"So how did the big proposal happen?" I asked, but wasn't

really listening to the answer. I'd suddenly decided to tell them about Will. Perhaps I felt the need to compete with Louise? There was the weird jealousy thing; I don't want Ed, but don't want you to have him either?

"…and then he just came out with it and asked me. So romantic! How could I say no." finished Louise and she pulled Ed's cheek like he was a small child.

He looked uncomfortable as he often did when I was around the two of them. A bit like when your mum shows you up in front of your friends when you're trying to look cool. I decided it was now or never.

"Actually guys, I've got some good news of my own. I might have someone to bring to the wedding." I said cheerily. Louise was straight in with the questions,

"Oooh exciting!" She ushered me into their lounge and patted the sofa as to where I was to sit and then quickly sat beside me.

"When did this happen?" Said Ed. If I wasn't imagining it, he looked a little hurt.

"You never mentioned anyone; is this a new thing?" He said. I felt like I'd somehow been unfaithful to him, which was ridiculous. I focused on his face as I told them the second part of my revelation.

"It's a bit complicated; it's actually a guy." I forced out. Ed was in disbelief and he stopped himself smiling when he realised I wasn't pulling his leg. There was a silence.

I couldn't bring myself to look at Louise, but she was the first to speak.

"Well that's a bit of a shock. When did you decide that you were gay then?" she asked.

There was that question again, *When did you _decide_ you were gay?'* Had it been a decision? Is that what had happened; had I made a choice to be gay? That implied that I could just as easily decide to be straight again didn't it? I felt like I was gay and had seemed to have lost any attraction to women. Maybe I had chosen to be gay in so much as I'd let the gay feelings come out of hiding. I was beginning to understand that perhaps I'd always been gay, but society had nurtured me to be straight. Now I was old enough not to give in to peer pressure but to be my own person, even if I was still scared of revealing that person to most people.

I was snapped back to reality by Ed going to get another drink. I told Louise that it was hard for me to explain and that I'd just fallen for Will, it wasn't about me being gay suddenly. Louise kept the barrage of questions coming and Ed sat in stunned silence agreeing with Louise whenever she said "Isn't that right Ed?" which she did often. When she was satisfied she had all the answers she needed she went to fetch the dinner from the kitchen.

I turned to Ed.

"You've not really said anything mate. You alright with this?" He put on his best smile but couldn't maintain eye contact with me.

"Yeah it's cool. I'm glad you've met someone new after Ruth. You should've brought him with you." He said nonchalantly.

I was knocked back by his last comment and was actually falling for his bravado, thinking I'd got his reaction all wrong.

"Yeah, well I thought it might be a bit odd to bring him without telling you first and I wanted to tell you face-to-face."

There was a silence as I debated whether to bring up the past. I couldn't imagine how this made Ed feel. Surely if I was straight and so was he, then what we did was pure experimentation, but if I was now saying that I was gay, would he be questioning if he was gay and living a lie? Would he be thinking that he'd done this to me after what we did? Maybe he'd be thinking that I was devious and had somehow used him because I knew I was gay all along? I wanted to ask him, but I couldn't because Louise had come back in with the food.

The novelty of my being gay wore off quickly for Louise who much preferred to talk about the engagement and forthcoming wedding.

"Now Ed, don't you have something you want to ask Gary?" She nudged him again. Ed still had a stupid grin on his face but was clearly somewhere inside his head working it all out.

"Oh yeah. Would you like to do me the honour or being my...,"

"Wife? But you've already got Louise. Oh I don't know Ed it's all a bit sudden," I joked. Ed looked horrified.

"No! I was going to say Best Man." He said deadpan. Louise and I looked at each other and she rolled her eyes as we laughed.

"I would love to." I said. I raised my glass.

"To the happy couple" I said and we all clinked glasses. Louise went on a rant about the wedding and kept insisting that Will should come too. I would worry about that when it came to it. Coming out to your friends was one thing, but coming out to someone else's family and friends was a different thing entirely, especially as Louise's family were gruff farmers from what she'd said.

As the night went on, the wine kept flowing and eventually Louise caved in and went to bed leaving Ed and I alone. It was all very polite but I felt like I needed to talk about the elephant in the room.

"So how you feeling about the whole me having a boyfriend

thing?" I said to Ed as casually as I could.

"I'm a bit shocked mate, to be honest, but it's cool. It doesn't change anything between us." He said.

"And you don't feel odd about what happened between us years ago?" I asked carefully. He looked uncomfortable.

"No, that was many, many years ago and it didn't mean anything." He looked like he was reliving a good memory as he smiled.

"We were just young and horny. Desperate even"

"You know how to make a guy feel special." I joked.

He seemed to be very philosophical about the whole thing and was very convincing that it didn't bother him at all.

We had one more drink for the road and went to bed – separately - despite one lingering moment on the landing when we said Good Night where I thought he was going to say something, but never did.

I lay on the rickety sofa bed feeling strangely satisfied. I had come out to both my best friends and it had gone pretty well. It was incredibly hard getting the words out but once they were out the relief was immense.

I had told my pals and my work colleagues, my family would have to be next, but where to even start?

Chapter 14

My mother is a typical Irish mother whose whole world revolves around her precious brood and our antics. My father is a former Army man who ruled with a firm hand as I was growing up and barely showed his emotions.

David is my eldest brother, then comes Paul, then me and finally Rachel came along; an accident five years after I was born. Growing up, I was well looked after, loved and beaten up in equal measure by my brothers.

Dad joined the army just after David was born and we moved around for a fair few years with his work. We grew up on military bases across the UK and in Germany too. Army life was surrounded by machismo; sergeants shouting orders; privates carrying heavy backpacks through muddy obstacle courses; tanks being raced. There were no openly gay people in my life (in fact gay people were only allowed to join the armed forces after 2000 and my father left the army back in 1992). I think by its very nature, the armed forces, attracts a certain type of man and then they train them to create soldiers: strong, non-emotive, competitive, fighters. Being gay was seen as the furthest from this macho image when I was growing up.

Funnily enough, neither my brothers nor I wanted to follow

our father into the army, yet my brothers would have certainly been more suited profile wise. They were both what you'd describe as lad's lads.

When my dad retired from the army, I was 12 and we moved to a sleepy small Hampshire town where they still live now. Everybody knows everyone else's business and any slight scandal became the talk of the town. I was a goody two-shoes at school and came away with good grades. I wouldn't say I was Mr Popular, but I had a good amount of friends... and girlfriends too.

When I was 18, I left home to go to university and ever since, when I went back to see my family, I'd shudder a little at how backward the town was. Seeing girls I went to school with pushing prams and dragging more toddlers behind them made me feel like I was lucky to have escaped.

I knew that I couldn't keep the fact that I was gay hidden anymore. It would have to come out soon and the family would all have to deal with the consequences; however bad I thought they might be. The fact is that it did feel like my day-to-day life in London was the norm and going to see my family in Hampshire was stepping out of that world and outside my comfort zone.

I love both my brothers, but they are very different to me. Both of them are very much red-blooded males who enjoy lager, girls and football. I, on the other hand, enjoy the company of girls as friends and, of course, partake in drinking, but apart from the aesthetics of certain players (Beckham and Torres for example) I've never been into football, or sport of any kind really. Because of this, I've been called a 'Poof' by my brothers on numerous occasions throughout my childhood. It was always just brotherly banter, but the implication again was that if you were gay you were some how a lesser man. Or at least that's how it affected me.

I think any serious thoughts they had that I might be a 'Homo' had disappeared thanks to my long term relationship with Ruth. Now, as far as they knew, I was single and had been for nearly two years. It was getting harder with each visit to answer their questions about who I was shagging or whether I had a girlfriend. I tried not to directly lie to them as such, but I did bend the truth, coming out with the standard phrases *"I've not met anyone special yet"*, *"I'm getting enough"* or *"I just want to be single for a while."*

My oldest brother David, was suspicious and his wife, Sue, definitely was. I remember on my previous visit to see the family, I was at their house with them and Paul, having a few drinks and watching a movie. Paul and David had gone to the kitchen to get some snacks, leaving Sue and I alone and she just came out with it,

"David thinks you're gay."

I just laughed nervously and said,

"What's he like?" I thought I'd gotten away with it, but she wasn't letting me off that easily.

"Because you've not had a girlfriend for ages and well he's always thought you were a bit of a poof, not into football and stuff." she said nonchalantly. I wasn't ready to spill my guts to her even if she was offering me an opening.

"That's just me. I'm fine on my own for now. I was with Ruth for over seven years and now just want to enjoy the freedom for a while." I told her a line I'd rehearsed many times. There was a brief nod from her as if she was going to accept that explanation at least for now. David came back in the room and we got on with watching a remake of Planet of the Apes.

Even though he was several years older than me, I had a good relationship with David. He'd always looked out for me when I was younger, whereas Paul was too cool for school and didn't like his little brother tagging along.

David and I would chat about music and films even though our taste, particularly in music, was completely different. He'd also taken me to the cinema many times in the past. To Paul, I was just a burden that Mum tried to put on him all the time and it wasn't until I'd gone to university that Paul and I had grown closer. Today we can chat about anything, well, almost anything.

David was becoming increasingly nasty to me lately, and every opportunity he could he'd come out with a little quip about me being a 'Gay Boy' or 'Poof' in what was supposed to be a jokey way. That night was no exception and Paul had picked up on it too. After we'd watched the film, Paul offered to drive me back to our parents' place where I was staying.

"Don't worry about David, he's just being a dick. We all know you're straight. I bet you're shagging the whole of London, aren't you?" he said. In my head I was screaming "NO! David is right!" but I just couldn't get the words out and wasted the opening I'd been given.

"Oh yes, there's plenty of the Gaz to go around." I said. Why couldn't I just tell Paul? I had the perfect chance, but fear had crippled me once again. It was that car journey that made me decide it was time to tell my family; I'd start with Mum.

* * *

That was six weeks ago and now here I was driving to my parents' house once again and my stomach was in knots at the

116

thought of what lay ahead. Surely my mum wouldn't have an issue with me being gay? I was determined to find out this weekend, one way or another.

After I'd gotten in and been force fed several cakes and a bottomless cup of tea, I asked mum if she fancied a drive out to the beach. This was something we often did. I missed not living by the sea and I think Mum just enjoyed our time together and a chance to chat without Dad in earshot.

As we strolled along the sand, I thought I was faking normal pretty well; smiley and happy, but inside there was a voice telling me that my confession couldn't wait. The fear was well and truly present.

We came to a stop and decided to sit and I absently picked up a stick and started making patterns in the sand as we both looked out to the sea gently lapping the shore. Mum was telling me that one of her friends was coming to visit from Ireland and how she'd have to get the house cleaned, or at least that was the last thing I remember her saying.

Suddenly, I felt lightheaded. My mind was going over lines like an actor rehearsing for opening night. How to say it? Should I go for 'Mum, I've got a boyfriend' or 'Mum, I'm gay.' Both sounded far too overly dramatic, but there's not many other ways to say it.

Mum had paused for breath and was looking at me as if she knew I was in deep thought. She went to open her mouth and stopped herself, clearly waiting for me to say something. A mother's intuition I guess. Panic shook me and I blurted out the first thing that came to my mind.

"How's Dad?"

"He's okay." Mum replied, with a puzzled look on her face.

"Good, good. And Rachel?" I added.

"She's good too." She lent in,

"Everything ok Love?"

I tried to speak but the words caught in my throat.

"It's not drugs is it?" Mum blurted out, then instantly regretted it.

"No….it's not that Mum" I said sternly.

There was a silence whilst she reached over and touched my hand gently whilst her eyes tried to find mine in reassurance. I could feel my dam of tears starting to crumble.

"Mum, I'm kind of seeing someone," I said quietly and I think she knew what was coming, because she left me to expand when usually she'd fire off a million questions.

"It's a guy. It's Will who you met at the pub quiz last time you and Dad came to visit." I waited to see what her response would be. Firstly, she gave me a reassuring smile,

"That's great Son. Does he make you happy?" She breezed it out as naturally as she could, but I could tell it had knocked her slightly.

You build it up to such a big reveal in your mind that when people don't appear to be shocked you're almost annoyed. I toyed with the idea of saying he was a lap dancer just to provoke more of a reaction. In this case though, I was just relieved at her response, but then a worried frown fell upon her face.

"Yes. He makes me very happy. He's ..erm…very different to Ruth." I said, unsure of where to take the conversation. This was new ground for me. I wasn't sure how to talk about Will and definitely wanted to avoid anything remotely sexual.

"I liked Ruth." Said Mum and I couldn't help but let out a little laugh as she clicked and tried to back track,

"But I'm sure Will is just as nice."

"He is Mum. I know you only met him briefly, but I think

you'll really like him. He's very laid-back."

"What star sign is he?" Mum asked with a look of genuine concern on her face, as if this could make or break our relationship. Again, I couldn't supress a laugh.

"He's a Pisces. What does that matter?" I said. Mum pondered a moment and her eyes went skyward as she mentally searched through the files in her head about Pisceans.

"Pisces and Leo, yes…I think that'll be alright. You bring the fire to make his water boil and if you get too hot he can put you out!" She said. I was now in fits of giggles; what was she talking about? Mum started laughing too and then gave me a big hug. I was overwhelmed by the love this woman had for me. Even though I'd thought she'd be okay with it, I still had the tiniest of worries that it might change things between us. I fought back happy tears as she looked me straight in the eye,

"Now, I don't want you to worry, but I'm not too sure how your dad will take the news." She paused.

"Might be best if you leave it to me to tell him. I'll be able to pick the right moment. You know how he can be."

"No! I need to do it myself," I replied before my brain had time to chicken out. My stomach filled with dread at the thought of it.

Mum put her arm around me.

"Well, let's not worry about that just yet. Tell me more about Will."

We walked arm-in-arm back along the beach and I filled her in on how different Will was to Ruth, that he made me happy and that he'd moved in with me. I think the last part startled her the most.

She revealed that she was suspicious that I was gay, but had never wanted to ask me or say anything in case I was offended by her asking.

The sun was beginning to set as we headed home. Although I was on a high at telling Mum, I didn't have the energy to tell Dad this weekend too.

In fact, my dad wouldn't be the next of my family to find out I was gay; my next coming wasn't one I had planned and one that I fought until I had no other choice but to come out…or risk the police getting involved.

Chapter 15

About a month or so after I'd told my mum I was gay, I was making my way home from seeing Kylie live in concert for the fifth time and well and truly had the Kylie fever. When I arrived at the train station, I had a 30 minute wait for my train so I called Will to pass the time.

"Hey baby. I'll be home at 11.50 can you pick me up from the station…Pleeeeeeease?" I begged and Will agreed.

"Aw thanks Sweetie. See you then." I put the phone down and looked around the cold and lonely train station. Hurry up train, I don't like sitting in the cold, even if I'd had a few warming drinks to get my body's central heating going.

Moments later my mobile rang and I was surprised to hear Will's voice again but now he was frantic.

"David's just rung the land line and I answered thinking it was you and you'd forgotten something." He was talking ten to the dozen.

"When I realised it was David I panicked and hung up."

Beep, beep. I'd just received a text.

"Well just don't answer it again if it rings and we'll pretend it was a wrong number." I said as calmly as I could.

This was exactly the reason why I needed to tell my family. It was ridiculous to think that Will could live in my flat but not be able to answer the phone and have to stay at friends should any of my family come to visit. This was his home now and he needed to feel comfortable in it. I ended the call with Will and checked my text.

'**Don't hang up on me!**' – it was from David. I texted back, '**I didn't hang up on you. You call on the mobile cos I was just on another call?**' He replied straight away '**No, at home**'. I thought I'd try the old wrong number trick '**I'm out tonight so you must've got wrong number**' but my brother had our family's stubborn trait and was having none of it.

'**Nope def ur number. I double checked and now no one is picking up.**' Shit! What could I say to that. *Beep beep.* Another text '**It must be a burglar.**' Oh no, I didn't like where this was going but I couldn't tell him, not like this.

'**Nah they wouldn't stop to pick up the phone would they. Must be one of those random crossed lines. You were probably talking to someone in Australia :P**'. Was that enough to pacify him? Not likely. His reply was this '**I'll call the police and get them to nip round and check it out.**' He wouldn't would he? I couldn't take the risk of wasting police time because I was a coward. '**Don't worry, I'll be back soon and can check for myself**' I replied, hoping that he'd calm down but it didn't work. '**No Gaz, I'm calling the police. You might not catch em if you wait til you get home.**'

I was panic stricken, I couldn't let him phone the police and waste their time. Would he really do that? I couldn't take the chance, I had to come clean.

'**No need to do that – I know who it is at the flat. It's my boyfriend.**' I hit the send button and felt the palpitations in my chest. I wanted to get off this train, I felt suddenly like a caged animal. I felt like I was in a life changing moment as I anxiously awaited his reply. A minute passed like an hour as I waited to hear my phone beep. There it was on my screen, a text message had arrived and I knew it could only be from David. Even though I desperately wanted to read it, I paused and felt a rush of emotion zoom up my body and prick at my eyes. My hands were shaking as I pressed to view the message.

'**Shit! So you're telling me you are gay? Why didn't you tell me sooner? We've been asking you for months.**' Was his reply.

Well at least he replied; that must be a good sign surely? I texted back

'**I just didn't know how to tell you. I'll call you when I get home.**' I needed to talk to him mouth-to-ear as it were, and not do this by text.

I reread his text to me as I sat on the train in a nervous trance. Surely he couldn't think his constant comments about me being a poof etc were him asking me if I was gay? I'd endured these kind of insults from him when I was a young boy, but took them for what I thought they were – just brothers ribbing each other. But the last few months he had gotten a whole lot more venomous. So why was my brother so aggressive and nasty to me? If he really thought I was gay, why not just ask me instead of giving me barbed jibes? Maybe it was frustration on his part because he just wanted me to tell him the truth? Or at least that's what I hoped. I was going to find out when I got home and called him.

I arrived home around midnight and read the text conversation to Will in the car. He couldn't help but laugh at the ridiculousness of David threatening to call the police. I was still anxious about the pending call I had to make and wasn't willing to see the funny side. As we walked in the door, I quickly ushered Will to bed. He had a habit of uncontrollably laughing when faced with serious situations and I wanted to be alone when I phoned David back. I pressed the button to dial his number and then quickly cancelled it before it had rung. I took some big breaths; I could do this, I had to do this. I dialled again, and launched into the conversation.

"Hi David. So that's my big secret out." I laughed nervously and so did he, then silence. What should I say now? This wasn't how I'd planned to come out to my brother, nor had I been in this kind of pressure situation. So far all my pals had been relatively easy and my mum was fine too. I think I knew deep down they'd all be fine, however with my brother - who'd been quite nasty with his taunts – I really thought it could damage our relationship. His silence wasn't allaying my fears right now.

"Sorry Gaz, just having a swig of beer." He said bringing some reassuring manliness to the conversation.

"I knew it! Didn't me and Sue tell you ages ago." He was quite smug in a told-you-so kind of way.

"Well it doesn't matter to me, Gaz, you're still my brother. I just wish you'd have told us sooner." He seemed calm and even sympathetic towards me. I was pleasantly surprised, but wanted to shout at him for all the recent gay digs. I decided to choose my battles and take his calmness for a win. Although he was my big brother and I looked up to him, we didn't really talk about anything emotional; it was all very surface level. Still, a huge tension evaporated from my body as I tried to open up to my big brother on the secret I'd sat on for a number of years.

"Have you told Mum and Dad?" He asked.

"I've told Mum and as you'd imagine she's pretty cool with

it but, I haven't told Dad yet." I replied.

"Yeah I can imagine you're not looking forward to telling him. Best wait til he's sober at least. If he gives you any hassle I'll sort him out for you," said David. There he was, being protective of me like he used to be. I felt a tear in my eye and a huge weight lifted. David added,

"Have you told Rach or Paul yet?" When I told him I hadn't he was well chuffed. Even in the face of this revelation he was still the usual David, wanting to get one-up on our siblings.

We chatted some more and again I felt the need to make it as a-sexual a discussion as I could, despite David making a few inappropriate jokes. As I put the phone down I was stunned at David's ease with the situation. I wondered whether it was all just shock and maybe he would turn nasty again, once it had sunk in. I chuckled as I thought of him loving the fact that he was the first of my siblings to find out: always competitive.

I dragged my exhausted body to bed. I snuck in and cuddled up to Will putting my cold feet on his legs, much to his sleepy annoyance. I fell into a tormented sleep – how would I tell my dad?

Chapter 16

I spoke to David a few more times over the next couple of weeks, not about anything particular, just general stuff. We were chattier than we'd been in a long time and he was instigating most of the contact, which was very unusual. I took this to be his way of letting me know that things were good between us and nothing had changed. I felt so relieved about that and also as he was the eldest, having him on side would help with my other siblings as we all looked up to him on some level.

It's ridiculous how desperately you fear rejection from those closest to you; your own flesh and blood, but you do. Telling them that you're different and something they have previously derided makes you so scared that you'll be disowned; your family, dysfunctional or not, is what you know the best. Perhaps in days of old that would have been exactly what happened – banishment.

I was an adult now and had made my own life away from the family, yet it's what it could do to the family that also scared me. Mum and David were both fine with it. Paul and Rachel should be too, but my dad, that was the ticking time bomb inside me that I didn't like to think about.

I decided to go for the lower hanging fruit that was my

siblings first. I felt an urgency to tell them now that I'd told David; it was only fair. Besides, knowing David he might beat me to it, then I'd be in more trouble for telling him first than for being gay.

Rachel would take it better surely? As a girl, I assumed she'd be much less bothered by sexuality, or at least that was my impression from the girls that I knew. Being gay seemed to be most threatening to straight men in my limited experience.

I decided to strike whilst the iron was hot and tell her on the phone. It's strange but even though I was the next oldest sibling to her, we weren't really as close as I was with my brothers. Her and Paul seemed to be closer probably because he had taken her out and treated her the same way that David treated me when we were younger. I think Paul now loved to think of himself as the big hunky brother that all Rachel's friends fancied; in his mind anyway!

I sat on my sofa, knowing that Will had gone out for the night. I picked at the slight tear that had recently appeared on the right arm cushion. It was a third hand sofa that had been given to me by a friend, whose parents had bought it new many years back. I absently twiddled the lose thread as I dialled Rachel's number.

"Rach, it's Gaz." I said in my usual silly yokel accent that we'd always put on with each other.

"Alright my luvver." She responded in the same voice "Oim jus in the car on the way to Mum's. What's new with the shrew?"

I was going to reply with the usual *'Nothing you need to know Schmo'* but decided that there was something new that this shrew needed to tell her.

"Well actually Schmo, I've got some news. I presume you're

sitting down if you're driving?" I said. She sounded excited,

"Oooh do tell then my luvvlie. I'm near pishing my pants with anticipation." That made me chuckle. I was almost acting a character (helped by the silly voice) as I dropped my bombshell.

"Well, it's that there brother of yours. You know the good looking one that lives up near the big smoke. He's only gone and got himself a boyfriend."

"No fucking way!" came another voice that wasn't Rachel's.

"Paul?!" I shouted, instantly aware that I gotten two for one with this coming out. He must've been in the car with her and she was on hands free.

"Yep it's me Gaz. So you're telling us you are gay?"

This was not what I was expecting at all; I was lost for words. I'd been prepared for a jovial conversation with Rachel where she told me she had already guessed and that everything was fine. Paul was a different kettle of fish and I would've wanted to tell him in a more serious way especially after him sticking up for me about David recently. An awkward silence followed.

"Well I can't say I'm not shocked Gaz." He said.

"I'm not! You always were better at doing my hair than I was," piped in Rachel who was, as I expected, taking it all in her stride.

"Yeah, sorry about all the sticking up for me you've been doing unnecessarily. I really wanted to tell you but..well...it's just...it's hard." I said sheepishly. I could feel a lump in my throat. I was choking up.

"I don't know what to say Gaz." said Paul. Not the kind of response I was hoping for. It's neither good nor bad and could go either way. I remained silent.

"I think what Paul's trying to say is we both still love you and it doesn't change a thing. Right bro?" chirped Rachel. There was a brief pause where I could visualise Rachel giving Paul a silent nod before Paul played along.

"Love another boy? You trying to say the gay gene runs in the family sis?" It was the start of what our family did best - take the piss out of each other. Paul had managed to push down his shock and revert to character. I couldn't stop the tears from silently running down my face; my family were instinctively protecting me.

The banter continued as I did my best to regain my composure as I chipped in,

"You just don't have the fashion sense or the personal hygiene to be a gay." We continued like this until they pulled up outside Mum's house.

"Listen Gaz, we've got to go, we've just got to Mum's." Said Rachel her tone taking a more serious air as she asked,

"Do Mum and Dad know?" I could hear Paul muttering in the background,

"I bet the old fart took it well," he said sarcastically referring to Dad.

"Mum knows, but Dad doesn't so best keep it that way for a while," I said.

"Ok well speak to you soon Luvver." Said Rach.

"Yeah bye Luvver!" Said Paul mimicking Rach and just before they hung up Rach said,

"Oooh almost forgot – you'll have to tell us all about this new fella of yours. I'll call you later."

I put the phone down and looked at myself in the mirror. Despite my tear-stained cheeks, I took a big exhale and there was my smile. It was a real shock that Paul was in the car, but it was a blessing in disguise – two birds, one stone. Of course, I'd still have to talk to them individually and explain it all and see if it had settled in properly, but for now it was two more off the list.

Mum called me that night.

"Your dad's in the bath," she whispered "I see you told you brother and sister then. How you feeling? Went okay, did it?"

There was a concern in her voice that only a mother can pretend isn't there and only a child can easily spot.

"Yeah, they both seemed fine about it. Did they say anything to you?" I asked, needing confirmation that I'd read the situation right.

"Well, Rachel told me in the kitchen whilst I was making the dinner, but Paul was in with your dad. Paul was a little quiet this evening but, he seemed happy enough. Oh here's your Dad coming.....and how's the job going?" She quickly changed the subject and then waffled at me for the next 47 minutes about her neighbours, the grandchildren and her friend Tricia.

Later that night, I couldn't face phoning Paul so I gave Rachel a quick ring instead.

"Hello Luvver it's me," I said.

"Hello you! So you've had a busy few weeks then. Mum told me about David – now that is too funny. Can you imagine if the police had turned up what would Will have done?" She adopted her best comedy London bobby accent,

"I em arressing you on account of you bein in a 'ouse what you shutant be."

"It doesn't bare thinking about." I laughed.

"On a serious note. How are you doing? This can't have been an easy time for you. David alright with it though yeah?" She said in her normal voice for once, which again got me in the throat – my family were all being so nice to me. I don't know why I expected them not to be, they were my family after all and that's what they do.

Maybe it's because they'd all grown up and still lived in a sleepy Hampshire village, where being gay was still definitely a gossip-worthy scandal.

"Gaz, are you still there?" It was Rachel's comedy voice back again to snap me back to reality.

"Sorry Luvver, I'd gone off in my own world then. These pills for my dementia see," I joked and slipped into my normal voice to be serious for a minute.

"David was surprisingly supportive and he's been texting and calling a lot more lately which I think is his way of showing he's ok with it, you know what he's like – keeps himself to himself mostly and usually it's me phoning him."

"Think yourself lucky. I live 15 minutes from him but I've not spoken to him for about three weeks as we keep missing each other at Mum's. Maybe I should call him tonight." The last bit more to herself than me.

"Tell me about your boyf then. Is he hot? Has he got a younger brother who isn't gay...but is still incredibly hot?" She said eagerly.

"Yes he's hot. No brothers or sisters I'm afraid but I'll ask him if he wouldn't mind sorting you out too." I joked.

"Urrgh you gays are so easy. You'll sleep with anyone." She goaded back.

"Don't put yourself down." I said.

"Oh gotta go Luvver it's my other luvver on the phone and he's hotter than you. Ciao!" And just like that Rachel was gone.

I checked my phone and was surprised to see I had a message from Paul, who must've phoned whilst I was chatting to Mum and Rachel. I listened.

"Hey Bro. I just wanted to say I am cool with everything. I

know I joke about poofs and all but it's just me having a laugh. Besides you're not like most gays who mince about and snog each other in public. Anyway, I'm here if you need to talk anything through. Actually why don't you bring your er… your partner to our engagement party next weekend. Mum and Dad won't be there and you can stay at ours so no worries there. No shagging mind….I mean not in the house as we'll have other guests. Alright Gaz, well speak to you in the week."

What a mixed message that was. I was pleased that he thought he was ok with it, but I just wasn't sure that he actually would be when faced with the reality of me and Will together in front of him. His tone had varied between jovial, guilt and warning in the message and I got the distinct feeling that he was happy for his little brother to be gay as long as he didn't have to see him being gay. Saying that, he had invited Will to his engagement party so we'd see.

* * *

"The whole family? Wow, you don't do things by half do you?" Will had just heard the news about Paul's engagement party.

"Nervous?" I questioned.

"I'm actually quite excited. We've been together for nearly two years now, and we're living together so it's about time I met your family properly. You've been annoying mine for months so it's only fair I get to return the favour." He teased and I pushed him on the bed and we wrestled a bit before it turned into a different kind of play.

Will's tune wasn't hitting quite the same notes as we drove to Hampshire several weeks later.

"Are you sure I look alright? How many people are going to

be there tonight? Who knows about us?" He was beginning to panic.

"Look, it's just Paul and Alicia and their friends. Rachel and Kyle too. Not sure if David and Sue will be over because of the kids. I spoke to Paul and he's told his mates too by the sounds of it so we can be as gay as we want." I said as I patted his leg and joked,

"Oh and remember you're not to try and shag me in the middle of the party." That lightened his mood as we laughed about how funny it'd be to dry hump each other in the middle of the room just to annoy Paul.

When we arrived, Paul and Alicia greeted us warmly and we could see the party was in full swing. Will and I chatted to a few of Paul's pals that I knew well and I could tell everyone was on their politest behaviour with Will, the usual banter reined back; definitely no gay jokes.

A few hours later, Will and I were stood in the kitchen laughing at a drunk girl who'd started a slanging match with another girl about her ex-boyfriend. We didn't think we'd seen such drama since school disco days. My future sister-in-law Alicia, was younger than Paul and I and this showed in the friends she was keeping. One of her many drunken friends came up to Will and I and started chatting away. She got round to asking if we had girlfriends – she obviously hadn't got the memo. I don't know if it was the drink or my confidence growing but I replied that Will was my partner.

"No way, you're winding me up. Kiss him then if he is." She said. I scanned the empty kitchen and nervously pecked him on the cheek.

"Rubbish, that's not a proper kiss. If you are together you would have a full on frenchie." She slurred as she prodded

133

me with her finger. Gauntlet down I looked at Will and our mouths made their way towards each other but never met due to Alicia's hand coming between them.

"Enough of that in here. What's going on?" with a look of panic in her eyes. Paul came in a split second later. The drunken girl spoke,

"Your brother reckons this is his boyfriend and..."

"Keep your voice down will you" butted in Paul. The drunken girl paid no attention (and I was actually routing for her),

"and I want them to kiss properly to prove it." She said with her head high in the air and slightly off balance.

"Well there's no need for that. I'm his brother and yes that's his, his...partner...Will." He ushered the drunk girl out of the room as she shouted "Snog him!"

"Right anyone for a drink?" Said Alicia and then she deliberately split us up.

"Will, you're good with the garden aren't you. Can I show you something outside?" Will gave me a knowing look and we both shook our heads.

A short time later, Will came and found me sulking somewhat in the living room.

"Ah, you escaped then? I can't believe how they reacted." I said, lip pouting like a grumpy child.

"I've a good mind to snog you in the middle of the room." My anger was simmering and I suddenly felt like being caustic.

"Let's do it." I challenged Will.

"I don't think that would be a good idea. As much as I'd love to see the look on Paul and Alicia's faces, I think we just need to behave." Will said, being the voice of reason. It wasn't what I wanted to hear.

"You do realise that if we were straight we wouldn't be having this conversation. How can Paul and Alicia pretend to be cool with us and then treat us like some dirty little secret?" I was getting more furious and felt like screaming to the world that I was gay. I think the alcohol had numbed my usual gay shame. Will was staying calm and clearly trying to talk me down.

"We just need to give them time. They've not known for long and they just need to get their heads around it." Will said as he fixed me with a pleading look. He didn't want a scene. He gently guided me outside into the garden where we were alone.

"It's your brother's engagement party and tonight should be about them." Will was nodding at me and I felt my rage subside somewhat; he was right. There was enough drama from Alicia's friends that I didn't need to add to it. I leaned in to kiss Will, for in that moment he'd reminded me why I was lucky to have him. He put his hand to my lips and shook his head,

"We can't. Come on, let's go and see what's happening in the other room at the live version of Jerry Springer."

I avoided Paul and Alicia the rest of the party as I was still seething, but I did manage to enjoy dancing with the drunken girl from the kitchen.

Next morning, I was still being frosty but no-one noticed as they were all hungover. We'd arranged to go to my mum and dad's place for a family dinner with David, Sue and my nieces too. Of course everyone knew they were meeting my new boyfriend except for Dad who just thought I had brought a friend home which wasn't unusual. I was excited for everyone to meet Will but also felt guilty that my dad would be left out and how I was sort of rubbing his nose in it without him knowing.

My Dad isn't a bad man and if you asked him for help, he'd go out of his way for you, but he is of a certain generation that seems to be void of emotions.

Growing up he was the scary parent and Mum was the soft touch. He had a fiery temper and you'd risk a slap if you didn't do as you were told. He has mellowed with age, although he still has a short fuse occasionally and can be very opinionated about things.

As we made the drive from Paul's to Mum and Dad's house, I was twitchy and Will was unusually quiet too.

"You okay?" I asked him.

"Yeah, bit nervous about meeting David and your dad." Will replied and I tried to reassure him,

"It'll be fine. You know my mum is a feeder and she makes a mean roast dinner."

"David has been nothing but nice since that night where he thought you were a burglar." I tried to lighten the mood by adding,

"As long as you don't steal anything he'll be fine." Will did break a smile at that, but was soon serious again.

"What about your dad? I do feel bad that everyone will know that I'm your boyfriend apart from him. Won't he go ape shit when he finds out?"

Will had made a good point, but what could we do? I wasn't about to march in and say *'Dad, I'm gay and this is my boyfriend. Pass the gravy please.'*, it was too late for that; we'd just have to ride it out. Now I was feeling nervous.

As we arrived we were greeted by Mum wearing her apron and a big smile on her face. She gave me a big hug and then went straight to Will and gave him a big hug too. Will looked a little shell shocked but returned the hug with a little less lustre than my mum. We were ushered into the lounge where Dad was sat watching the horse racing, but soon stood to greet us.

"Hello Son. How was the party?" he asked as we did an awkward hand shake.

I suddenly went blank and felt like the fact that I was gay was written all over my face and Dad would instantly throw us out of the house. Will must've sensed my freeze and quickly thrust out his hand to my dad,

"Hi John. Remember me from the pub quiz last year when you came to visit Gary?"

Whether my dad did remember him or not I've no idea but he was certainly playing along when he said,

"Aye. I told everyone the capital of Peru was Lima but you wouldn't listen," he laughed before telling us to sit down.

I felt like I was walking on egg shells, trying to analyse every sentence in my head before saying it out loud. I was glad when David, Sue and the kids arrived. I got big hugs from the kids and a punch in the arm from David; some things never change.

David gave Will an overly firm handshake, perhaps to show his manliness and introduced himself and his family. It was all very polite and I couldn't sense any tension in the air other than my own state of panic.

As we sat around eating Sunday dinner, Dad was winding up the kids and making bad jokes, always with half an eye on the Formula 1 on TV of course. Sue and David saw their opportunity and started to ask Will questions.

"Seen any good films lately? I really want to see Mistaken Identity" said David.

"Not heard of that one. What's it about?" replied Will.

"It's a comedy about a guy who is having a secret affair and the cops think he's a burglar." Said David, with a grin.

I nearly choked on my lunch but Will styled it out.

"Ah yes now I know. The lead actor is the one everyone fancies right?" said Will. David seemed impressed by his quick wits.

"Yeah I think all the girls might fancy him but I heard in real life he's gay." said David. Sensing he'd maybe gone too far, Sue jumped in,

"He is a handsome guy and whoever lands him is lucky."

This was a surprisingly tactful and flattering comment from Sue, I was shocked. I quickly changed the subject and dinner proceeded without a hitch.

After dinner, Will had gotten the thumbs up from the family and had actually got on fine with my dad. As we talked in the car on the drive back home Will said,

"I don't know why you lot take the mick out of your dad so much. He seems fine to me." I couldn't stop laughing.

"Wait until I tell David and Paul about this."

"What?" said Will.

"Why is that so funny?" He gave me a dig in the side.

"Ow!" I said and continued to laugh.

"Well you're seeing the good side of him. You try sitting with him when he's had a few more drinks."

"What about the rest of the family?" Will asked.

"Sue said to me in the kitchen that you were lovely. Don't worry I soon put her right." I teased.

"I have to admit I was really nervous about meeting them but I think it went okay. Did I do well? Huh? Huh? Did Will please master?" The latter being said in his best servant Igor voice, complete with rubbing his head against me like a pet.

"Well I can't believe you let rip at the dinner table but..."

"That was the chair!" Will protested. Either way, it had given us all a good laugh at lunch, much to his embarrassment.

"David scares me a bit. There's an edge to him." Will paused. "Don't get me wrong he was fine with me but he just didn't look comfortable."

"I think he's trying really hard to accept that his little brother is gay and like Paul it's easy to pretend that everything is cool whilst I'm up in London, but when it's in their faces they're forced to deal with it." I said. Will looked thoughtful, so I lied and added,

"He told me that he thought you were a really nice guy and I'd done well." Will sat up and beamed.

"Well you know he did follow me into the toilet and ask for a blowy, but I told him I needed to let my dinner go down first."

We carried on like this all the way up the motorway but then moved onto the more serious situation of me coming out to my dad.

"When are you going to tell your dad then? It's one thing for him to think I'm your friend but another to find out I'm molesting his son. Do you think he'll go mad when he realises that you've flaunted it under his nose without telling him?" Will asked. I felt a darkness coming over me.

"I feel genuinely bad about today," I paused,

"I just don't know how I'm going to tell him. He's so stuck in his ways and we just don't talk about anything emotional so how do I bring it up?"

My inner thoughts were pouring out in semi monologue form now.

"Hi Dad, who has won the Formula 1? Oh did I mention I was gay?" Can't see that going down too well." I gave a big sigh. "I just don't know how I'm ever going to do it." Will ruffled my hair.

"Well don't worry about it right now, we're nearly home and safe in our little bubble for a while longer. You'll do it when the right time comes".

Will was right; no point worrying now. We parked up outside the flat and were instantly back in Gary Land where I was safe and my secret wasn't a problem.

Like a nagging in the back of your mind every time you leave the house (*'Did I unplug the iron?'*) I was plagued by a little voice in my head saying *'Have you told your Dad yet?'* at least once a day for two weeks following that trip. The pressure I was putting on myself was building and a trip to see my parents alone needed to be next on the horizon.

Chapter 17

It was nearly my mum's birthday and I always go home to see and pamper her; she loves nothing more than having her family around her. I told Will that I would be going alone and he knew that meant I was going to out myself to my dad.

It was also Football World Cup season, Ireland were playing that day and my dad and David said they were going to the pub at lunchtime to watch the match. I'm not really into football, but a weird ladishness takes over when it's the World Cup or Euros. I think it's because everyone gets so fired up and patriotic, making for a great atmosphere. It's also a short period of weeks so you can get behind your team and watch a few games without having to know that much about the players or whatever offside is. Plus it was a great bonding chance for me, Dad and David.

We made our way to the Red Lion and happily downed pints as we watched Ireland put on an uncharacteristically good performance coming out of the game 2-1 up. The atmosphere in the pub had been fairly quiet when we arrived, but we'd soon whipped up a storm and were shouting and cheering at the screen. We left the pub and I think it must've been the alcohol that had given me a bravery boost and an urgency to tell my dad that I was gay. That soon disintegrated as we walked home and passed a teenage lad sporting black nail varnish.

My dad instantly made some limp wrist gesture and called after the poor lad,

"Oooh Hello Nice Boy" – he was a goth and I doubt he was gay, but to my dad it was all the same. David and I then had to hold my dad back as the lad gave him the finger and called him a wanker.

This knocked the wind right out of my sails and I felt scared, ashamed of myself and my dad in the same instance. I felt sick and must've drained of colour because David's voice woke me from my trance.

"You alright Gaz? Oh no, you're not going to chunder are you?"

I got it together quick sharp. My drinking ability, and thus my macho credentials, was under threat. As if I'd ever be sick from drinking alcohol?

"I'm fine, was just thinking about something I've got to do for work but it's gone now. That was some match eh? Keane really shone for me." I said trying to sound football savvy. Dad burst into his match summary,

"They were jammy shits. If I'd have been the manager I'd have put Finnan on much earlier and played a 4-4-2 formation. We'd have won by even more if they'd done that." To which David and I just rolled our eyes and let him waffle away, with David making rude gestures behind his back and me trying to look interested and not laugh.

When we got home the room was beginning to close in on me. The angry voice was at me again *'DO IT! What are you waiting for?'* If he kicks you out you can go and stay with David tonight. *'GET ON WITH IT!'* came the voice in my head.

Mum was looking at me with concern; her maternal senses kicking in and alerting her that something wasn't right with me. I gave her a look that she knew meant not to ask me here.

"Do you fancy a wee walk in the forest Son?" She asked and I leapt at the opportunity. As we walked towards the forest we chatted and I told her about David taking the micky out of dad on the way home and how I'd had to focus really hard not to laugh in his face. It was when we stopped at a bench that I burst. The tears streamed down as I admitted defeat about not being able to tell dad.

"Come on Son, don't get upset. The time will come and then it'll be done, but I don't think with you in this state and him with a few drinks inside him, that today is that day." She was wiping the tears from my eyes and moving my chin up so that I was looking her in the eye.

"It's not worth getting yourself so worked up about. Now come on…..and ever so slowly the corners of his mouth began to turn." She'd gone and used her underhand Mr Happy trick that had made me smile ever since I was a little boy. We sat arms around each other on the bench, probably causing some controversy with the dog walkers who passed. Was that Sheila James with a younger man?

The rest of the evening passed without incident with Dad in high spirits or should that be high on spirits? Whichever, the three of us played cards and had a good laugh, and I got up early the next day and headed back to the safety of my flat and Will.

Two days later, I was in Tesco's bagging up some broccoli (and giggling like a school boy at one particularly knob shaped courgette) when my mobile went.

"Hello Son." Came a very sombre voice. It was my mum.

"Hi Mum. Everything alright?" I said with concern as she was unusually downbeat, normally it was like a beam of sunshine coming down the phone when she rang. I feared that someone had died.

"Has something happened?" I said anxiously.

"No, no. Everyone's fine. I'm just ringing to tell you that I've told your Dad."

BANG! Someone had run into me with their trolley as I stopped in shock. I had to get out of the supermarket right away.

"Hang on Mum." I said as I battled my way out of a blur of people leaving my trolley and shopping for another time. I realised I was holding my breath so the fresh air felt cold against my lungs as they refilled.

"Hello." I said trying to sound cool "How did he take it?" I could hear Mum's mind thinking of the best way to phrase it.

"I think he's a bit shocked and it's going to take some time for it to sink in, but he did say that you were his son and that he'd never be ashamed of you." I could feel tears welling in my eyes, even in the shock he'd shown a real pride toward me; something that he'd never shown to my face.

"Anyway, it's done, so stop worrying about it now. I've not told him about Will yet and he did say that he wasn't sure he could cope with you bringing anyone home with you, but it's out in the open and we'll get through it. Okay? Well I'd better go." She said. I was dumbstruck, but managed to sniffle out,

"Okay. Oh and Mum, thanks." It was the one I'd feared the most and I hadn't done it myself – Papa had a brand new fag!

I couldn't face food shopping so drove home and cracked open a bottle of wine. That was a good response from my dad right? I started to beat myself up – I should've told him, he'd have thought more of me for doing it. Been the bigger man and all that.

Who was I kidding? I'd had a lucky escape. I stopped arguing with myself and took some deep breaths, sipped the wine and numbed my brain with some meaningless TV. I'm sure the next time I saw him and explaining that Will was my boyfriend would be another mammoth task, but at least step one was complete.

Chapter 18

My next work assignment was T4 on the Beach (a big outdoor pop music concert with lots of different acts) and that's where I met Carl; he scared me a little from the moment we met. He was a journalist who was interviewing all the stars as they came off stage. I was chaperoning Lee Ryan when Carl collared me and asked if he could grab a quick interview with him. I got the all clear from Lee's people, but was told he was going to grab a quick sandwich first, so I got stuck with Carl for about 20 minutes while we waited.

A tall guy with dark brown hair shaved severely at the sides but left long on top giving him a floppy fringe that covered one of his eyes. He had a bad habit of flicking said hair off his face with a carefully executed head manoeuvre. He wore clothes that all seemed to be a size too small despite him being rake thin; he was an instant bleep on my Gaydar. He was very camp in both his mannerisms and the way he talked – things I usually ran a mile from, yet I found myself warming to him. He was a pop music fan just like me, in fact much worse than me.

We were soon having a good old chat, talking about this one and that exchanging funny celebrity stories and discovered a mutual love for Kylie. Well it's always nice to meet a fellow Kylie fan, especially a purist who had been a fan since I Should Be So Lucky and The Loco-Motion days.

Before long, Lee Ryan turned up and Carl got on with the interview. I have to say that he was a brilliant interviewer, definitely knew his stuff and was actually flirting with Lee. Lee, who I'm sure has a big gay following due to his boyish looks and his boyband background, was playing along with it too. I felt like shouting "Get a room!" I was in awe of Carl's self-confidence and how comfortable he was with his sexuality. I wished I could be so forthright.

After the interview Carl and I chatted some more and it turned out that he was covering another T4 event that I was working on in two weeks, so he asked for my email address. I was a little bit nervous about giving it to him in case he thought that it was my way of saying I was interested in him, but I gave it to him anyway as I joked,

"If my boyfriend knew I was handing out my email to complete strangers, he'd kill me." I wanted to make it clear I was taken. He actually seemed to look more excited by this comment and stroked my arm as he said

"Don't be silly dear, he's got nothing to worry about." There was something in his eyes that first set my alarm bells ringing. He was like the archetypal gay old man I'd seen in a few comedy films who walks a thin line between flirting and sexual harassment. Carl, was actually a couple of years younger than me, but we certainly had lots of common interests. We said our goodbyes, I shook his hand very formally and off I went with Lee to the stage area.

I travelled home on the train exhausted after running around after various pop stars all day, making sure they were suitably pampered and on stage at the right time. The day had been fun but very long and I still had an hour long journey in front of me to get home to a nice, long soak in the bath. I'd recently been given my first Blackberry for work and thought it was brilliant being able to check emails on the go. Now, as I flicked through a full inbox, I realised that it was just another way of extending the working day.

I started looking for emails from friends rather than work stuff and also found it a good time to delete all those *'Sorry for office wide email but does anyone have a Nokia charger?'* or *'Purse found in first floor ladies loo'*. Plus the oh-so-funny comebacks too; *'It must be Mike's purse that he left when he was doing his make-up'*. I was quite surprised to see an email from Carl so I opened it.

Had my suspicions been just? Was that a sinister twinkle in his eye? The note itself was pretty harmless. He just said that it was good to meet me and would be good to have a drink sometime, chat all things Kylie and that I should bring Will along. This last bit made me relax. You wouldn't be trying to pull someone if you invited their boyfriend along too, surely?

I sent a note back saying that would be good and suggesting he drop me a note next week with some date options.

He didn't wait until next week however, he pinged me straight back. He just started general chit chat about a classic 80s film he was watching, Earth Girls Are Easy. I'd never actually seen it and he went off on one about how he would have to lend it to me because it was a 'so bad it was good' kind of film. The conversation went back and forth in emails of one or two paragraphs and before I knew it I was pulling in to the train station, so I signed off and went home.

As the week went on Carl's emails kept coming as we got

to know each other better. Carl seemed to have similar views to me on the relationship front. He was single, but looking for love and didn't want to just sleep around. He wanted the movie style big 'fall in love' moment and to have a monogamous relationship with one special guy. Where this special guy was is what was eluding him at the moment. He didn't seem to ever have had a boyfriend as far as I could tell.

We put a date in to meet for a drink and I mentioned it to Will but after what I'd told him about Carl, he knew he was in for a night of Kylie talk so he opted out. I felt completely relaxed about meeting him but was thrown off a bit by his greeting and his choice of location. I hadn't been to the bar before and it was instantly obvious on arrival that it was a gay bar. I was petrified. My only previous venture into a gay bar whilst at university hadn't gone well.

The décor was quite dark and dingy but with the odd neon flash and I wasn't sure if it was paying homage to the 80s or hadn't been decorated since then. There was a central aisle, almost like a catwalk, that led straight from the door to the bar. I walked in very fast, scanning the room for Carl but trying to make no eye contact with anyone. I felt that everyone was looking at me – not because I'm hot, but because all eyes seemed to follow me. I'm guessing that it's part general nosiness and part perving? Even those who appeared to be in couples seemed to stop talking to look you up and down.

That's one of the things about being gay; you and your partner can both fancy the same person. Can you imagine a straight couple watching a guy coming into a bar and the girl saying *'He's hot.'* Her boyfriend would probably be raging and very unlikely to agree. Saying that, if a girl said the same about another girl, her boyfriend (having to choose his words carefully) would probably have a different reaction entirely. Something like *'Maybe the three of us could have a little fun tonight?'*

I was beginning to really lose my confidence as I paced back towards the door. I was just about to do a runner when out of the blur of men pops Carl who grabs me as he says,

"Come here you big hunky man." as he goes in for a hug. I must have looked like a rag doll as I just froze. What did the hug mean? Was this how gay friends greeted each other? I sat down shell-shocked as he went and got the drinks in.

He sat down a little too close for my liking.

"No Will tonight?" he said with a raised eyebrow. *'Get out of here!'* shouted my head but then I looked at the crowded path to the door and all the gribbly older men, in their tight vest tops, morphed into hyenas with drool hanging from their mouths as they checked out the latest young pup to enter the bar. I felt like I'd stepped into the bar in From Dusk Til Dawn. No, the better option was to stay at the table with Carl, I would throw him to the pack and save myself if it came to it.

I plonked my small rucksack in between us to give me a bit of my own space back and took a big gulp of my beer before replying to Carl's question.

"Will sends his apologies. I didn't realise but he'd arranged to go out with one of his pals tonight so he said he'll meet you next time."

"Oh well, at least it means I've got you all to myself," he said with that look in his eye again as he patted my knee. He was like a panto dame; he really was. I was really uncomfortable with him touching me but I think that was just how he was; a very camp and tactile person.

I downed my first beer in just a few gulps.

"Someone's thirsty!" said Carl. "Shall I get us another?"

"Same again please." I said. I was relieved he was going to the bar, but as soon as he left I felt vulnerable. I'm sure it was all in my head, but I felt scared to make eye contact with anyone for fear they'd come on to me. I was relieved when Carl came back with the drinks.

"Oooh have you seen the arms on that bar man? He can squeeze me to death with those any day" he said.

"I hadn't noticed," I mumbled and I really hadn't as I'd been staring at the floor. Carl noticed that I was looking a little uncomfortable and put his hand on my knee again.

"Don't be scared. I'll look after you" he said. I wasn't sure whether I should be more worried about him or the bar. I subtly managed to manoeuvre his hand off my leg. I wanted to know how someone could be so comfortable in themselves about being gay.

"Can I ask you when you knew you were gay?" I said.

"Darling, I don't know what you mean," he said before an over the top laugh and a sip of his gin and tonic.

"But seriously," he continued.

"I think it was obvious to me and everyone else that I was gay when I was about 14. I had such a crush on my Maths teacher, Mr Kennedy, he was dreamy."

"So your mum and dad knew when you were a teenager then?" I asked.

"God no. My dad left my mum when I was only 2 and I've not seen him since and my mum still doesn't know." He said.

I nearly spat out my drink. How could she not know? He was very camp. Carl read my mind and elbowed me.

"Oi! Well of course she must know but we've never had that discussion and it's not like I have someone special to take home to introduce her to" said Carl. He looked sombre for a second as his mind drifted off.

I was thinking that it must be really difficult to deal with the fact that your father doesn't care enough about you to stay in touch or want to see you. I was beginning to think that Carl's chirpy, dramatic, camp exterior was actually hiding something a lot more confused, hurt and vulnerable. I was just about to dig a little deeper when he startled me with the line,

"When am I going to meet that someone special. All the good ones, like you, are taken".

How do you respond to a statement like that? I wanted to make sure that he knew there was never ever going to be anything between us, yet he was now my friend and needed comforting words.

"There are plenty of nice guys out there, you just have to look for them." I saw an opportunity to have some fun.

"Come on, let's scour this place and see if there are any potential suitors for Prince Carl in here." He laughed and put his arm on my knee again.

"There you go again always saying the right thing. You haven't got a brother have you?" I did have a brother, two in fact but they were likely to give him a different kind of pounding than he wanted.

"Who do you like in here then? What about him by the bar?" I said, ignoring his comment and shifting my knee a little so as to make him move his hand. Carl looked round the bar and was beginning to get quite excited by this new game and soon started pointing rather unsubtly at various hot guys around the bar. It soon became apparent to me, however, that he had very high standards and I'm not sure how I can say this in a nice way, but he was pricing himself out of the market, so to speak.

These were the very, very handsome guys with amazing buff bodies that clothes hung off like catwalk models. I felt perhaps he needed to be more realistic; you'd have to be Brad Pitt to try and pull these guys, but you never know - maybe I was jumping to conclusions and not giving these guys a chance. Just because they were stunning didn't mean that they necessarily wanted to only date fellow supermodels. Carl had a great sense of humour, maybe he could laugh his way into their hearts...and their pants? Maybe not.

"Ok then, if you're serious about finding a boyfriend why don't you go and talk to one of them?" I proposed.

"Oh Lord no, I couldn't possibly. What would one say?" he retorted, pinky finger erect as he sipped his gin and tonic.

"Quick, that cute blonde has just gone to the bar...." I necked my beer, "...and I'm fresh out of beer. Would you be so kind as to get me another, darling?" I mimicked him by raising my pinky finger too.

"You are terrible Gary. Ok, wish me luck," he smirked.

"Bottoms up!" I quipped.

"There will be nothing going up my bottom!" He said snootily, as he sashayed to the bar.

It was like watching a reality TV show. I tried to look inconspicuous as I saw Carl squeeze himself next to the beefcake at the bar and open his mouth to speak to him. The blonde didn't even seem to notice, he was too busy checking himself out in the mirror behind the bar.

"Well that was a waste of time," moaned Carl as he returned to the seat with our drinks. "I asked him where him and his friends were going later and he said him and his boyfriend were staying in here."

"Ouch! Ok one down and about forty to go." I said hopefully, raising my beer to clink with his glass.

"Suddenly I'm not in the mood," he said glumly. "It's late and I should be getting home. Got some research to do for my Lisa Scott-Lee interview tomorrow."

I used Carl as a human shield to make my way out of the bar and as we stood outside, I was ready for our goodbyes and quickly put my hand out to shake his. His pitiful face suddenly switched to naughty imp as he put both his hands out and said,

"Oh come on now. Give me a hug – I need one after that brush off." I gave him the quickest manliest hug I could, then mumbled goodbye as I rushed off in the direction of the tube station.

Why did he insist on making me feel uncomfortable? What was he up to? I didn't entirely trust him, yet we'd had really open and honest conversations and he knew how I felt about things like that, and that I was in a happy monogamous relationship. He claimed to respect everything I said and have the same moral codes, but why couldn't I shake the suspicious feeling?

* * *

The next month, Carl had blagged four tickets to an exclusive Kelly Clarkson one-off gig and my name was on one of them. I was so excited but knowing that it would be a late night and I would struggle to get a train home, I asked if I could stay at Carl's place. He of course accepted saying I could sleep on the sofa. However, as the date came nearer he told me that two of his pals were coming too and would be staying at his place. I wondered where we'd all end up sleeping and took my sleeping bag with me thinking I might end up having to just find a piece of floor space in the living room. I didn't mind; I suspected I'd probably be quite drunk and sleep where I fell.

The concert was good, but a bit strange in terms of the people I was with. We'd met up with another group of Carl's friends (one of which Carl seemed to have a twinkle in his eye for) and I was left feeling a little alone and out of the clique. I was glad to bump into my pal, Ebonee, at the show and ended up going closer to the stage with her, much to Carl's disgust, but I was there to see the show not try and cop off with someone. Besides, his pining over this Australian guy was too much and I felt like a clinger on. At the end of the show I found Carl still doe-eyed at this big Australian friend-of-a-friend.

"We're going to Heaven" he said. Great, another gay bar; I was quite apprehensive but I had no choice. Luckily, I managed to persuade Ebonee along, as I was feeling annoyed at Carl, and the rest of the group who were still being cliquey. Ebs and I danced the night away and turned my initial frustration into a great night out. Carl emerged later looking furious at me and disappointed that the Australian wasn't interested in him. I said goodbye to Ebonee as Carl, his two friends and I headed back to his flat.

His two pals were staying in the living room and I was going to sleep on Carl's bedroom floor: this wasn't the plan and I immediately felt uncomfortable. Glances were exchanged between him and his best friend as Carl announced this, and I didn't feel at all comfortable, but what could I do? I'd missed the last train by now. I got my sleeping bag out and laid it on the floor.

"You don't need that. You can share the bed is a king size."

He said flippantly.

"I'll be fine on the floor thanks." I mumbled. He tried to protest but I was having none of it. Then came the bit I'd been dreading; I had to get undressed.

I felt like he was almost salivating with anticipation as he pretended not to look as I pulled my jeans down to reveal my boxer shorts. I did it as quickly as I could and then jumped in my sleeping bag, zipped up and faced away from him. I imagined his eyes boring into me, and his hands floating just inches above me once I'd gone to sleep. I wanted to beat the living daylights out of him. How could he make me feel like this? How could I have been so naïve to think that it wasn't his plan all along to try and seduce me? He started talking to me.

"Do you know I think the other two are getting it on in the living room. What a pair of tarts eh?" I had heard noises too and assumed the same. I felt like Carl was trying to suggest we should be doing the same and I was fuming. I wanted sleep to take me now, make it morning and get me the hell out of there.

"Yeah. Listen I'm knackered. Night." I closed my eyes and prayed for sleep to come and that I'd wake unmolested. As it was, I barely slept for the fear.

Morning brought an awkward atmosphere. The other two guys seemed to be a bit sheepish because they knew we had guessed what they had been up to and I was really cold with Carl as his best mate was giving him a look as if to say *'Well? Did you two get it on?'* I made my excuses and was out of there as soon as I could.

I checked my email on the way home, as had now become habit on the train, and there was already a message from Carl about it being a good night etc. I didn't respond. I needed to put some distance in our friendship.

'**Hello???? Anyone home??**' came his text the following day. I didn't know how long I could ignore him without going into a whole confrontation as to why I was ignoring him, especially because prior to that we'd be emailing most days about nothing in particular. I was also questioning if I had misread the situation; was it all in my head?

'**Sorry. Things have gone mental at work with that new show; I'm having to work all the hours. Hope you're well and let's catch up in the next few weeks.**' I thought that was a suitably vague response that would get me off the hook for a while. Boy was I wrong!

Not less than five minutes after the message was sent my mobile started ringing; the caller ID showed it was Carl. I couldn't face talking to him so let it go to answer machine; he left no message. Shit. What did he want? I pushed the thought out of my mind, I had just started work on a new TV show. It was another dreary reality show to find the latest children's TV presenter.

I was on my way to the studio to work on some storylines with the contestants, you know the sort of thing '*I'm doing this for my mum who's only got one leg after being attacked by a mad sheep on our farm*' and '*I want this so much. Growing up I always wanted to work with children and entertain them, especially the handicapped ones.*'

The crew were all set for Jonny Wiggles (no, not his real name, but one the producers thought would suit him better), the mood had been set and we even had an onion on hand should the tears not flow naturally. Then my mobile rang. It was Carl again – second call of the day and again I put it to voicemail and then switched off my phone. I made my apologies to the disgruntled contestant who clearly didn't like a minute of the limelight being taken away from him.

Another two hours of stories ensued with each contestant claiming to want it that little bit more desperately than the last. Then it was lunchtime. I switched on my mobile to give Will a call about tonight's dinner: I really had a craving for curry. To my surprise I had seven missed calls – all from Carl. Still no message. He was doing this on purpose to arouse my curiosity. I checked my Blackberry, but no new emails from him on there. I'd have to call him. What if it was something serious? His phone was ringing.

"Ooooh Hello Mr Unavailable. Too busy to talk to the likes of us commoners now are we?" came the snooty greeting.

"Hi Carl, is something up? Like I said in my email I'm on shoot all this week and rushed off my feet. I see you've been trying to get hold of me" I replied completely ignoring his catty opening gambit.

"I just wanted a chat. Did you see Lost last night? Can you believe what happened to the gorgeous doctor?" He was back to normal now as if I'd phoned him for a chin-wag. I could feel the anger rising.

"No, I didn't see it as I was working as I told you and I don't have time to chat now either. I'll catch you later in the week." I said quickly adding, "I've got to go. Bye." I hung up before he had a chance to retort. I put the phone down and started on my sandwich, but before I'd even swallowed my first mouthful the phone started ringing. Guess who? I put it straight to voicemail. Yet again he left no message. About five minutes went past and then my phone rang again. This time it was a different number that I didn't recognise so I answered in my best businesslike manner, in case it was work.

"How dare you hang up on me! How rude, I've never in my…"

I hung up again. It was Carl. He'd fooled me by ringing from a land line. I was fuming but couldn't suppress a little chuckle at how mad I knew he'd be for me hanging up on him again. I switched the phone to silent and started to look through my emails.

Ping! Carl had emailed me. Now I knew from past experience that he marks all his emails with a read receipt, so he'd know if I'd opened it or not. I did however have the benefit of autopreview so I could at least read the first few lines without him knowing:

What is your problem? How rude. I've never had anyone hang up on me twice in one day before. I thought we were good friends. I don't understand why you're being so vile. You never used to be like that. I'm going to

He's going to what? Damn me and my curiosity. I couldn't resist could I? I was going to read on and then I'd be forced to reply. No. I could resist. Let the stupid idiot stew for a few hours. I'd bury myself in work and then go home to Will and a nice curry. It bugged me all afternoon, but I didn't have to read the email to find out what the next bit was.

It was 7pm when the day's filming was finally done and I wearily made my way to the exit, only to find Carl sat in reception waiting for me with lips so pursed you'd have said they were more like a handbag. This is all I needed.

"Oh there you are. I thought you were never going to come out." He projected like he was on stage at the Old Vic. I was furious. What did he think was going on that he could turn up at my work and cause a scene in front of my colleagues. I ushered him towards the door with a face like thunder.

"Aren't you going to introduce me to your colleagues. Oooh you're cute, hello." He said over his shoulder as I pushed him

159

out the door.

"What are you doing here?!" I rasped in a shouted whisper (if such a phrase exists). "I can't believe you'd turn up and embarrass me in front of all my colleagues. What do you want?" Carl's usual high camp sneer and overt confidence seemed to shatter as a vulnerable, hurt soul stood in front of me. A split second later the bravado was back,

"I can't believe you are having a go at me when you, YOU!" he prodded me, "are the one who's hung up on me and ignored my emails. I came down here so you could apologise to me." That last line was like a red rag to a bull.

"Well you've wasted your time. It's you that should be apologising to me. I thought we were friends and I've made it clear that I'm taken!" I thought I saw Carl roll his eyes at this point and it was enough to send me over the edge.

"You and your ...dirty little friends all just want to sleep with each other and I'm not interested! When will you get it into your head that I'm not interested in anyone else than Will. Especially not a camp Freddy like you!" I'd gone too far, but it was too late.

"Goodbye Carl," I whispered as I tried to hide my guilt at what I'd said. I'd been really, really harsh and I knew it. Carl wasn't a bad guy, I just think he didn't understand my insecurities when it came to being gay.

It's not like him and his friends were hurting anyone, who was I to judge them if they all slept with each other? Wouldn't I have tried to catch a sneaky glimpse of the guy I fancied in his boxer shorts too? Maybe I'd gotten it wrong and he didn't fancy me at all.

I felt terrible for what I said and started writing an email apologising, but then deleted without sending. I had to put some distance between us otherwise he'd be smothering me again. As badly as I'd handled it, the result was the best for both of us; I don't think I'd be hearing from him again.

Chapter 19

Much time had passed since my dad had learnt I was gay and despite his initial reservations about me being able to bring a boyfriend home, my mum had told him about Will and I and persuaded him it'd be alright to let Will come down for the weekend. I knew it would still be a struggle with him going forward, but at least everyone wanted to be ok with it, even if it was going to be hard at times. I felt so lucky to have such a loving family; for being accepted. The fear of rejection that goes with having to come out is horrendous.

I was nervous at how he would feel about the obvious deceit from Will's previous visit, however, he didn't seem to hold that against me, and despite my trepidation as I walked in the house, Dad was actually more animated than I'd seen him in a long time.

Mum was there to give both Will and I a big hug, but Dad had also taken to his feet and was standing behind her waiting his turn. There was an awkward touch on my arm as he said hello, then he shook Will's hand and said hello, encouraging us to follow him into the living room whilst Mum put the kettle on (and plated up countless cakes).

"Good journey?" asked Dad.

"Yeah, only took about two hours." I replied.

"That's good then." Said Dad

"Gary tells me you're a tennis fan," Dad said to Will. I certainly hadn't told him that, it must've been Mum.

"What do you make of Team GBs chances at this year's Davis Cup then?"

I didn't even know what the Davis Cup was and don't think I'd ever heard my dad talk about tennis. I was stunned that he was making such an effort and felt my eyes start to get watery.

Will seemed to relax instantly, giving me a 'what were you worried about' look. I was in shock. My dad was doing this for me and I felt very touched indeed. Feeling it was safe to do so I went to the kitchen to help Mum and whispered,

"*What's gotten into him?*" She just shrugged and we both laughed as I gave her another big hug.

* * *

Will and I had been living together in my small flat for a couple of years and had decided to look for a house together. It felt a bit scary because a joint mortgage is just as much of a commitment as marriage really. I kept the fear at bay by thinking of it as purely a business deal and a sensible one at that. I had to pinch myself at the things that had happened in the last few years. There I was coasting along with a boring office job, living with my girlfriend and starting to talk about kids and a mortgage, and now a few short years down the line, I was working in TV (something I'd always dreamed of), had my own flat and was looking at getting a joint mortgage with someone of the same sex. Kids? Who needs them! I'm not a selfish person and I'm actually really good with kids but 30 minutes with my nieces and I'm ruined. Children are a joy I'm sure, but I've seen too much lately of what happens to the parents. They either become so exhausted they are like zombies or they become worse – Parentzilla. A disease more likely to affect the mother from what I've seen, making a conversation with a Motherzilla nigh on impossible. Firstly, they are usually running around after their child or sat watching their child's every move rather than concentrating on what you're saying. Many a time I've said things like *'My dad's dead'* and *'my testicle got so swollen I had to have it amputated'* and got *'Umm hmm. That's nice'* back.

Secondly, when they do talk to you it's often in a patronising tone that they would use to talk to their child or worse, they are showing off about their spawn.

For example I'd say,

"Ha ha look she's collecting all the yellow balls" and Motherzilla would reply,

"Yes she does that. It's apparently because yellow has been found to remind them of the womb" or something equally banal. I know that if Ruth and I had gotten around to having children she could've easily become a Motherzilla and I'd have found excuses to get out of the house a lot.

It does make me sad, however, to think that I might never look at a child and see my eyes looking back at me (that's if you don't count one of them playing with my glass eye when I'm older). I know Will thought he wanted to have children until his friends had them (or was it when he met my nieces?) and he realised how much you have to give up your own life to look after them. I wouldn't be surprised if he felt some kind of duty on his shoulders to carry on the family name. My oldest brother has three children, so less pressure for me, but with Will being an only child, of parents who were both only children, the buck stops with him. For now though, our baby would be our new house and so the search began.

The house buying process is painful and it occurred to me that there were some things that a same sex couple would have to deal with that straight couples wouldn't. Firstly, there was the usual embarrassment of the advisor trying to guess whether we were a couple or just pals buying a house together. Then we discovered we were among unusual company when it came to the life assurance questionnaire. *'Are you any of the following: Smoker? Haemaphiliac? Homosexual? Mass Murderer? Child Molester? Etc.'*

Ok, so maybe it wasn't quite that bad, but I was seriously stunned to see that we were in a category with people whose blood can't clot. Will was braver than I and said *"Yes"* pointing to Homosexual and then the advisor looked at me and didn't need to ask; I just smiled and gave her a nod.

"Right, that's everything done, but the life assurance people may be in touch as sometimes you have to have tests. It's random, but I just want to make you aware now," she said efficiently. Well, you can imagine our surprise when it turned out we'd both been 'randomly' selected to have a HIV test. Who'd of thought that was going to happen? It made me really angry. Just because we were gay they had decided that we were higher risk of being HIV, no doubt because we slept around and had unprotected sex with anyone and everyone. I hate being stereotyped, especially when in this case they couldn't be further from the truth.

What's even more annoying is that they don't even tell you if your test was negative, they just say if there's any problem they'll contact you. You have to just wait until they approve your policy. Every day after the swab test, I nervously eyed the post just in case, even though I knew there's was no way it could be positive.

With the paperwork done it was on to house hunting, snooping round people's houses and deciding whether they were for us or not; that's the fun bit. Those we did look at, I tended to let Will lead the way and look more like a friend who was with him for a second opinion. I hated the thought of these strangers judging us in case they had any prejudices that might not make them want to sell to us. I was being very paranoid. Besides they'd find out we were a couple if we liked the place enough to make an offer.

After a few properties fell through, it was part desperation, part luck that a house came back on the market that was in the area we wanted. It was a lovely bay windowed semi-detached house in our price range and the original buyer had fallen through and the sellers were desperate to not break the chain. The décor was horrendous; I'm talking pink, purple and yellow doors and gloss work. Who in their right mind would do that? Even for a child's room let alone the bathroom and the master bedroom, but I liked the challenge of doing it up and putting our stamp on it.

After weeks of frustrated toing and froing, finally the day arrived and we went to pick up the keys to our new house. A place that was jointly ours. We'd been getting on fine in the flat but ultimately it was my place and no matter how accommodating I was, I knew that Will felt he was more of a guest. As we did our first lap of our new house, we stood in the back bedroom and both felt so excited and so content as we hugged. It was one of those moments you could live in for the rest of your life. *BING BONG*. It was the front door.

Will's parents were there beaming away; I think his mother might've been even more excited than us. Our perfect moment was lost but the joy remained with us as Will delighted in showing his parents around our new home. His mum gave us lots of suggestions about what carpet we should get, as his dad pointed out some DIY jobs that needed doing. There really is nothing like walking into your new house for the first time and soaking it all up, feeling proud and excited about the home you're about to make it into. Will came into the garden. We had a garden! He handed me a glass of champagne that his mum and dad had brought with them. Well, I say glass, it was actually a mug as we hadn't unpacked any glasses yet.

More importantly it was only days before my birthday and I'd arranged a house warming/birthday party for the Saturday; lots to be done before people arrived. This is one of my worst habits - giving myself stupidly tight deadlines, especially for a party's sake.

Later, on that first night as we started to unpack, the doorbell went and it was our new neighbour, Alan, with a bottle of wine. He was in his 50s and reminded me a lot of a smiley Arthur Fowler from Eastenders. This was a nice welcome to the neighbourhood. It was me that answered the door and I introduced myself as Will came down the stairs. There it was; the look of non-comprehension on Alan's face as he tried to work out which of us lived there, if we were related or if we were a couple. He didn't seem phased for more than a split second and neither Will nor I were helping him figure it out. The next day Penny and Paul, our other neighbours, knocked on the door with another bottle of wine, but this time it was only Will that was in as I was back at the flat getting more bits together. Will's mother was also at the house so they ended up not sure who was actually living in the house either. We invited both neighbours to our house warming party and they both turned up for a quick drink. They actually seemed like really nice people and although I didn't come out and explain we were a couple, it was obvious, if not from us, from the way our friends talked about us. I remember Ebonee saying something like *"I used to work with Gary and so met Will through him."* And Dan saying, *"We often go away on holiday the four of us."*

The fact was that we didn't really have that many gay friends so the party was a fairly straight heavy affair. Several weeks later, we'd become good friends with the neighbours and Paul revealed that we had caused a bit of confusion in the street when we'd moved in, with different names floating about – Cary and Will, Gary and Willis and so on. One neighbour even thought that Will and his mum were a couple!

Despite being gay, we are actually surprisingly light on gay friends. I think this is partly due to living in suburbia and not being very scene focused, but also because I think a lot of gay people scared me. I don't really embrace being gay as a way of life, I just see it as being my sexual preference and nothing more. Just because I'm gay doesn't mean I have to change my friends and only hang out at gay bars. I was quite happy with my suburban life with the good friends I had, the house and the life partner. However, I wasn't averse to meeting new friends whatever their sexuality and being gay was an instant thing in common I had with other gay people. I have met some very interesting gay people in the last few years.

* * *

Sian was a girl I'd met about a month ago when I started working on another musical linked reality show. She was a really vibrant, energetic girl who shared my love of fooling around. We hit it off instantly and become the jokers of the team, always dancing about or doing silly accents. I felt so at ease with her and we had become inseparable at work, and started going for drinks regularly too. I could sense that other members of the team were gossiping about us and thought we were getting it on. They couldn't be further from the truth.

It was actually within the first half an hour of meeting Sian that I'd come out to her. She wasn't shy about asking direct questions.

"Do you live with your girlfriend then?" She asked, and I surprised myself with my automatic response,

"No, I live with my boyfriend." After it had come out I was instantly looking for approval, but I was to be surprised again by her response.

"Oh you're gay? Me too." She said. I was getting a glimpse of what it was like on the other side of the coin. I didn't know anyone who was a lesbian. You do feel a bit flustered, like you should say something but you're not sure what to say. I chose "Cool" as if it was some sort of hobby.

I then relaxed and found out that her girlfriend was called Clare and they'd been together for over four years. The conversation turned to lighter things and we got on with getting to know each other and working together. I wanted to ask her the questions that I'm usually asked – did you always know? How did you meet your girlfriend? How did your family take it? etc. Now I had a new understanding of the reactions of my friends and colleagues whom I'd come out to. Then was not the appropriate time to ask such questions, I'd wait until another time.

Meeting Sian made me realise that however much you think you're completely open minded to something, when it's actually in front of you, you soon realise that you have certain prejudices. Sian completely blew away the stereotype of the butch lesbian who wears dungarees and comfortable shoes that is often portrayed in the media. Well, she did like wearing converse and was a bit more tomboyish, but she had long dark hair and olive skin (on account of her father being Egyptian) and was very pretty.

She wasn't what a lesbian looked like according to the preconceptions in my mind. I chuckled at this thought as I caught myself and it sunk in that the same thought process was probably being undertaken by some of the people I'd come out to. You start by thinking that they're not fitting the stereotype and then you start to exaggerate certain qualities (like the tomboyishness in Sian, or maybe people would look at my more show-off side and label it as a gay flamboyance) almost as if to allow your brain to comprehend it. *Ah hah, yes they are gay; I can see that now in the way he knows all the moves to Steps latest single.*

John and Juan (whom I lovingly dubbed the two Johnies), were the next to become great gay friends of mine and proved that monogamy can exist in a gay relationship. They've been together for about 7 years now and Will and I always joked that we're watching their relationship to see what's coming next for us.

I met John through Sian actually, although they were more passing acquaintances. They'd worked together on a previous project and we bumped into him and a pal in a gay bar in Soho. I remember being on edge as we entered the bar, as I often was in gay bars. Sian had lapped up the scene lifestyle and would often go to mixed (guys and girls) gay bars. This particular night was impromptu drinks after work and it was Sian who casually mentioned going into Form, a bar that she knew. It was quite funny as the ground floor bar was full of groups and same sex couples and we walk in arm in arm. The barman actually said to us,

"There's another bar upstairs." Which puzzled us. Then Sian understood where he was going with this one.

"He thinks we're straight," she whispered to me. That made me relax and we started playing up hugging and stroking each other and being soppy.

"No we're fine down here, aren't we Snookums?" I said. He looked like he was going to be sick – which made us play up even more. It was as we moved away from the bar that I saw a guy waving in our direction. I panicked and turned to Sian trying to move her in another direction, thinking he was waving at me but she pushed me round.

"Oh my God! It's John who I worked with at the BBC. Come on." said Sian. I couldn't believe my ego and sniggered to myself hoping that Sian hadn't clocked what had just happened or I'd never hear the end of it.

We sat down and I was introduced to John and his friend Ben. Sian and John were catching up as Ben and I sat in silence listening to the conversation. I physically relaxed when I heard John mention that they were meeting their boyfriends later who had gone together to see Morrissey, someone that both John and Ben would rather die than go and see apparently. John's dramatics made me laugh and he looked at me.

"Well would you?" He asked.

"Most definitely not!" I remarked. This turned the conversation to music and John and I found we had similar taste and started getting overexcited reminiscing about Five Star and Kylie. Sian rolled her eyes and grabbed Ben to go to the bar she knew we'd be chatting for ages and indeed we talked all night, exchanging email addresses at the end. Then Sian dragged me off to a club called Ghetto, where we danced the night away until Clare turned up and got in a huff because we were being silly. That put a dampener on the night and we left not long after that.

Next day I had an email from John which just said *'Stick or twist? The choice is yours'* (a lyric from a Kylie song). I replied *"I will confide. What do you want to know?"* And so the emails started; we began chatting regularly and arranged to meet up for a drink. The situation was very similar to how things had started with Carl and I was a little wary, however from the way John often mentioned his boyfriend I didn't think I had cause to worry. I was getting none of the vibes I got from Carl.

When we met for a drink it was again in a gay bar, but through my friendship with Sian I was going out a bit more on the scene, so I was getting more confident and less scared. I still hated going in alone though, but now I went straight to the bar and ordered a drink then looked for friends from this vantage point.

John was running a little late. I sipped my drink slowly when I recognised a familiar face coming towards me. Before I had time to escape, Carl was in my face. I acted surprised as if I was pleased to see him.

"Carl, Hi!" I could feel the awkwardness engulfing me,

"How are you? Good to see you." I blurted as if he was an

old school friend, but I'd said the wrong thing.

"Good to see me eh?" He smiled and there was that nasty twinkle in his eye.

"Come here." He gave me a big hug and said,

"Oh I've missed this face." He pinched my cheek like an old uncle does when seeing their five year old nephew.

I was embarrassed and stunned at both the hug and the cheek grabbing. I wanted the floor to open and swallow up me. Better still if the room could open and swallow him.

"Fancy seeing you in here." He said with a menacing raised eyebrow.

"I didn't think you liked these, what is it you said; 'seedy' places?" His smug demeanour was making my skin crawl.

"I don't, but I'm meeting a friend," I said, as friendly as possible. His face looked intrigued and a bit put out as John arrived.

"So sorry I'm late. Can I get you a drink?" John puffed out, he'd clearly ran to get here.

"No. We've got to go, our table is booked for 5 minutes time." I said turning my back a little to Carl and winking at John before he blew my cover.

"Huh hmmm" coughed Carl unsubtly. I did my best 'silly me' impression as I introduced Carl, quickly saying,

"Well, glad to see you're doing well. Best go, me and John are off for dinner and we're going to be late." I walked away trying not to appear too rude and I don't think I was paranoid when I say that I could feel his eyes burning into my back – especially the lower end of it – as I walked away.

I filled John in on the embarrassing situation with Carl as we made our way to another bar. John shared a lot of my concerns and dislikes of gay stereotypes but seemed completely happy in his own skin. We spent the evening non-stop chatting. This time, alongside debating pop music we got on to the subject of our other halves and I explained about Will and I, and how things were going really well. He surprised me by telling me that he met his boyfriend Juan over seven years ago and they had been together ever since. He was just 18 at the time and Juan was his first and only boyfriend. Juan had wooed him when he was studying in Madrid and the two had just hit it off from the start after a mutual friend introduced them.

Listening to other people's coming out stories was a real tonic to me. It gave context to my own struggles and also made me grateful at how my family and friends had been. We instantly shared the experience of being gay and having to tell our loved ones and society too, yet each of us had different tales to tell.

Chapter 20

There must have been something in the air as wedding season seemed to have hit and we had a packed summer of love ahead.

On a gloriously sunny day in June, we rose to our feet in the most grandiose of churches as the first hymn started. About half of the congregation stood perplexed as the other half started singing at what seemed to be the wrong time, but was in fact correct. Clearly some of us were believers and others, like me, not so much; at least my skin wasn't burning as I'd feared.

As the song went along, I couldn't stop from giggling as sentences and words were sung in such a random way. Some long and drawn out, others squeezed in so awkwardly. It really was guess work. I was stood next to Will's pal Dan; we'd actually become close friends and he was now pretty accepting of both the gay thing and me. In fact, we had been on holiday with him and his girlfriend Suzy just last month.

As the organ puffed out another dodgy off-tune note, Dan caught me sniggering and that set him off too. By the time the line 'Purple headed mountains' came we had tears streaming down our face and our shoulders were shaking. The people behind must've thought we'd been overcome with emotion.

The bride's mother however clocked us and flashed us a scathing look that wiped the smiles off our face. Well until the next hymn that is.

This wedding was Will's friend Mark, who I'd actually warmed up to slightly too, although was still nervous of him when he was drunk. Will and I joined the convoy plodding out of the church accompanied by a dodgy organ version of Love Is All Around. I suddenly felt a bit nervous as I didn't really know that many people.

Will hadn't noticed. He was too busy whispering to Richard who was one of his old school friends. A very good looking guy actually and I didn't like the attention Will was giving him. Or maybe it was the lack of attention I was getting from Will that annoyed me. I was feeling very exposed, like I had an arrow pointing at me saying 'Wedding Crasher'. I'm sure it was all in my head, but it was there alright. I felt like everyone was wondering who the hell I was. I stuck close to Dan and his girlfriend Suzy as we were joined by Craig and Glen, who went to school with Dan, Mark and Will. Dan introduced Suzy as his girlfriend then looked a bit lost for words when it came to me so I just stuck out my hand and introduced myself as a friend of Will's. I could tell they hadn't been told about Will being gay and they seemed quite content to keep chatting to Dan. I stood there with a fixed grin on my face as if I was listening, but it's boring when old friends reminisce about old times and people you don't know.

I scanned the crowd for Will and not surprisingly found him stood laughing in an over the top way at what Richard was saying. I'll kill him! I thought. My mood was about to get worse as the official photographer called all Mark's school friends and their girlfriends for a photo. Dan grabbed Suzy and strode off with Craig in tow. Assuming that I wouldn't be in the photo Glen asked if I could look after his camera. I accepted with the best smile I could manage. I wanted to go home. Will had waltzed over to the group photo with Richard and hadn't even thought to look for me. Still I would have my revenge as just as the photo was taken, Will clocked me looking daggers at him and his face dropped and was certain to have been caught on camera.

It really is awkward when you're part of a couple that is only partially out. It feels like such a big statement to make to people you'd not seen in about 15 years and were unlikely to see again for another 15. I knew my jealousy over Richard was just my insecurities manifesting themselves, but I was angry that my partner in crime wasn't by my side. In my mind, it was Will's friends that we were mingling with and he should be the one to out us as a couple; not me. For Will it was just a good day for catching up with old friends. He was in his element, but for me there was that feeling of not fitting in again.

After the photo he made a beeline for me and with his best smiley voice said,

"There you are. Why didn't you come in the photo? I couldn't find you." The cheeky bastard.

"Yeah too busy looking at Richard. Nice of you to finally notice I wasn't around." I said angrily. Will went to defend himself but Glen turned up and my face automatically went full smile as I happily gave him back his camera. Will was all sweetness and light and joked away with him.

"Hey Glen. How are you? I see you've met Gary my…er…" Will's tongue had acted quicker than his mind and I waited to see what he would say.

"…friend from work." He said. Glen explained we'd already

met and then the two of them had one of those conversations peppered with the awkward pauses of people who realise they've nothing in common but their past. *You work for a silage company you say? How interesting, do tell me more.*

"Oh looks like everyone's heading off to the hotel now for the reception" said a relieved Glen as he rushed off leaving Will and I.

"I really am sorry." Will said to me .

"Friend from work, am I? Is that how we're playing it today?" I asked.

"I'm sorry it just came out. I am proud of you... of us. I don't know what's wrong with me today I guess it's being round old school friends has made me slip back into playing the role I did when I was at school. I suppose I'm scared of what they might say which is ridiculous as I barely see them. Also it seems pointless to create a fuss especially when it's Mark's big day." Will said as I kept silent. I knew what he meant. I hadn't told my ex-girlfriend and didn't offer it to any of my old school friends on the rare occasions when I'd met them.

"Plus Glen was always been a bit of a lad's lad. I guess I bottled it," said Will. I knew how hard it was and could completely understand especially if Glen was more of a blokey bloke; they are the hardest to come out to. Will sneakily grabbed my little finger with his and said,

"Come on, let's go and enjoy the rest of the day."

"Ok. Let's go get drunk," I said and tried my best to forgive him despite feeling insecure.

"Should be champers at the reception, I hope?" I took a deep breath, painted on my smile again and tried to let go of my tension.

"If there's not, I'll eat the groom's top hat! Mark's from a very wealthy family so should be the proper stuff. No cava in sight." Will added with hope in his voice.

The hotel was amazing. Beautiful antiques and gold leaf everywhere including the ceiling of the banquet hall which looked like the Sistine Chapel (or at least how I imagined it to be – we hadn't gone in when we visited Rome the previous summer as the queue was too big.). I pounced like a cat on a mouse to grab a glass of champagne from a cute passing waiter. We found Dan and Suzy and the four of us stood taking in the amazing surroundings, Richard walked over to us arm in arm with a woman I assumed was his girlfriend. Will turned to introduce me and once again I held my breath as I waited to see if he would out us or go for the easier route of co-worker.

"Richard. Olivia. This is Gary.." said Will before being interrupted by the maître d announcing that the bride and groom would now be greeting their guests. The moment was gone and that was as far as that conversation was going to go for now. As the crowd moved towards the entrance, I saw that it was a line up with the parents of the bride and groom alongside the couple themselves. I shot a questioning look at Will and whispered,

"Who am I if the parents ask?"

"Just say you're a friend, but I'm sure they won't ask. Make a comment about it being a lovely day and move on," replied Will just in time. The queue was moving swiftly and I could hear Mark's mum let out an excited squeal as she said hello to Dan. My heart was pounding. Will was greeted just as warmly from Mark's mum and then came my turn. I saw her mask slip slightly when she didn't recognise me and couldn't match me to either Will or the elderly couple behind me. But it was only for a split second. This was a high class professional socialite;

no doubt the head of the women's institute in her village.

"Beautiful ceremony. You must be so proud." I said with a Cheshire cat style grin and swiftly moved on to the father of the bride, giving him the same line. I felt like I'd barely taken a breath so when I finally reached the bride I was overcome by the massive hug she gave me. She certainly had no concerns over the fact that I was gay and probably revealed it to half the guests when she loudly said,

"Gary! So nice to see you. It's brilliant that Will found you. You make such a lovely couple." I felt my face go instantly hot and knew that my cheeks had flushed.

"Beautiful ceremony. You look lovely." I robotically spewed out and gave another scary grin. I couldn't bring myself to look at the couple behind me, the parents or even Will. I sort of froze on the spot, only to feel Will's arm around me as he pulled me forward to get another unexpectedly big hug; this time from the groom.

"Maybe you two will be next eh?" said Mark. Sensing my utter horror at being asked that, Will laughed and moved me along.

Will was laughing as he grabbed two glasses of champagne from the cute waiter's tray.

"Trust those two to do our dirty work for us."

"Is everyone looking at us?" I said without moving my lips. I took a big gulp of the champagne and nearly choked as it went down the wrong way. Will was in hysterics as he pushed me out into the gardens.

"You ok?" He finally asked. Then he shocked me by giving me a big hug as he whispered in my ear,

"I love you Gary James." Looks like wedding fever had gripped him. I pushed him away like a child does when their

180

mum tries to clean their face with a hanky and a bit of spittle.

The next wedding was Will's best friend Tim from university. This one had the added twist that Will was Tim's best man and so I was left to introduce myself to most people whilst he busied himself looking very self-important. It was my turn to bottle it and I had to be outed as Will's boyfriend by the girlfriend of another university friend who I had latched onto for protection. As Will stood up at the altar in the church, I felt proudness swell up inside me. He looked so cute in his tails, as he turned and winked at me. I think it was my turn for the wedding effect to take over. Looking around the church it was like a scene from a soap opera; everyone in the congregation looking at each other with doe eyes and dopey smiles, squeezing the hand of their partner or making eyes at that guy or gal they fancy. Will was giving me *'Awight Tweacle'* eyes and I returned his look with *'I love you'* and then I looked round the room, head held high as if to say *'that's my man up there'*.

Will had learned his lesson from Mark's wedding and pulled me into the photos and generally kept an eye on me all day. I hadn't learnt from my killer hangover and began quaffing the wine at the reception. Once more, ending up spending most of the night making a fool of myself on the dance floor – my Irish jig is now becoming legendary, if only I could remember doing it!

Once again the oldies got a bit confused and kept hinting that Will being such a lovely young man would be the perfect match for the chief bridesmaid. Will and the bridesmaid played along for a bit although she was fully aware of our situation. I thought I'd spice things up and pretended I was after the bridesmaid which shocked Auntie Maude into action as she cut in on my dance to whisk me away. I could see Will bent over with laughter as the old dear waltzed me around the floor as far away from the bridesmaid as possible.

* * *

The third wedding of that summer's trilogy (*let's call it Bored of the Rings*) was my brother Paul's, but first we had the stag do to get through; a lads' trip to Faliraki. I was dreading it. Everyone else on the stag do was straight, it wasn't even a consideration for one of them to bring their wife or girlfriend, but Will was invited, probably for Paul not knowing what to do about him and wanting to be inclusive. He certainly wouldn't have wanted to go on Alicia's Hen Do, but we talked it through and agreed that it would be best for just me to go on Paul's stag do. I was glad he did, because I wanted to do this one by myself. Will had been on both stag dos for his friend's recent weddings and I'd gallantly let him go on his own, now it was my turn.

He would however, have to put up with several of the guys at our house the night before we flew though. My brothers Paul and David, plus Paul's friends Ian and Nick all came to stay and that's when I realised what I was letting myself in for.

It was a Friday afternoon and I'd taken the day off work to be there when they arrived. No sooner had they barged each other through the door and dumped their stuff than they all said in unison, '*Let's go to the pub!*' and off we went.

David was the ring leader being the oldest. He was enjoying the freedom of no wife or kids for a few days and was going to take full advantage of it. He got five pints and five shots and took several large gulps before declaring a pool tournament.

I could keep up with the banter, even got off on it, but the drinking pace was fast and I wasn't sure if I could last a whole long weekend in Faliraki.

I was rubbish at pool but that didn't matter so much as we ended up playing two against three with David once more taking me under his wing to thrash the other team.

We moved onto another pub and then another where David started a round of dares. Paul took the lead for a while as Nick was dared to try and pull the barmaid and Ian had to stand on the table and sing 'I Will Survive' (one that was originally intended for me but David told them no and they listened thankfully). The pace of drinking had slowed and I felt relatively sober compared to the others. That's when I got a surge of testosterone and demanded we do tequila slammers. Yuck! I hated the things. What was I thinking? Perhaps I was more drunk than I thought. I also decided that I'd succeed where Nick had failed and after some smooth talking I came back with the barmaid's number and the shots. The guys couldn't believe it and so they dialled the number and I won't repeat what they called me when they saw her pick her phone out of her bag. Let's just say it started with 'Jammy'. I tried to grab the phone off Paul as he put on a stupid voice and said,

"Hi! It's that guy you just served. I couldn't tell you this at the bar but I've only got a small willy," and hung up. I daren't look at her. What was I playing at? It was the alcohol giving me my 'I don't care jacket'. I felt smug and was showing off to my brothers that I was as good as them despite the fact that I was gay. The hang up was still there for me and I didn't want to feel like a lesser man somehow. Their attention turned to taunting Nick for failing where a 'Gay Boy' succeeded. I actually liked

183

them taking the micky out of me that night for being gay. That meant they accepted me; in the same way that Nick was always called Slick Nick; I had a new nickname that was somehow affectionate rather than offensive this time. It had taken a little time, but both my brother's genuinely seemed at peace with me being gay now.

I started to think about the barmaid. Why was it that I found it easy to talk to her and to chat her up, but put me within five metres of a gay guy I fancy and I'm out of there or turn mute. Now that I'd revealed my amazing 'talking to women' talent, for the rest of the night my dares seemed to involve talking to a group of girls, before the rest of the group charmingly joined me. Nick (being the dog he was) ended up going home with one girl and I think David and Paul were both incredibly tempted but I reminded them about their wife and fiancé respectively and they looked like children who are desperate to do the one thing you've just told them not to. I half expected David to grab the girl's boob whilst looking at me to see if he'd get told off, but instead he settled for a hug and a cheeky feel of her arse that he didn't think I'd noticed. Where was Ian? Oh God there he was at the bar trying to chat up my barmaid. I couldn't face seeing her after the phone call so I sent Paul in to get him.

"You still got her number Gaz? She's well fit I might call her when we get back from holiday," said Ian. The four of us stumbled into a taxi and after verbally abusing the taxi driver over the cost of the ride, I managed to get them home. Will was fast asleep – *was* being the operative word. My brother's thought it'd be hilarious to all get in bed with him much to my protests. So in they climbed and snuggled up to him before pretending to bum each other. Will pretended to see the funny side of things, he had to, he was still a little scared of my brothers, especially when they were drunk and unpredictable. I managed to get them out of the room and thought that it would be time for bed, but they had other plans and opened more beers. I left them to it and next morning awoke with a killer hangover to find them sleeping soundly with lots of empty cans and bottles around them. They'd drunk the house dry including a melon cocktail that someone had brought to a party about two years ago. It made me worried how I was going to cope on the trip, but I'd just have to do the best I could. I tried to get the lads up as we had to get ready for the flight but they weren't moving. Luckily the doorbell went at that moment. It was Nick looking rough, but happy.

"Not had much sleep Gaz," he told me as he tucked his conquest's knickers in my dressing gown pocket. Urrgh! He was walking up the stairs taking off his top.

"Alright if I jump in the shower?" he said as he started undoing his jeans. He was such a flirt and I didn't know where to look.

"Sure go ahead. I've got to try and wake this lot" I said turning slowly away.

"Gaz, quick look at this!," he said and as I turned round he had pulled his jeans and boxers down to his knees giving me a full frontal view.

"Perv!," he said as he laughed and I turned away flushed. Suddenly I was seeing some benefits of the trip. Looking isn't cheating and I had a feeling that with twelve lads on tour I was going to be seeing a lot of man flesh in the coming days.

What can I say about the stag do? Nada. What goes on tour stays on tour – as we kept being told by Paul. I can tell you that I was a good boy as was the groom, but certain other members of the group weren't quite so well behaved. Plus Paul most definitely doesn't suit union jack dresses or like having his balls waxed – something I couldn't stay in the room for. No one wants to see their brother's scrotum. Ian managed to find a distraction to the barmaid and David realised he didn't have the stamina for drinking like he used to.

I'd done it – I was as much one of the boys as the next man. In fact being gay actually gave me a special place in the group. Not only was I the lady bait again, but I was also a novelty and well looked after. I'm not sure my liver will get me past 35 now but I'm glad I went and I just hope that my mum doesn't ask me too much about it. It is ridiculous how when you put a group of straight men together it gets a bit primal and the testosterone makes each of them jostle for position and try to prove they're more manly than the next.

I'd gotten through the stag do and was now looking forward to the wedding. My only slight issue was how to explain Will to my aunts and uncles who were none the wiser about my sexuality. I had a few months yet to worry about that.

Chapter 21

'*Eileen will recover fully. Eileen will recover fully. Eileen will recover fully. Eileen will recover fully*'
I wrote this over and over on my pad as a fought to hold the lump in my throat down and stop the teary dam from breaking. It was a power of positive thinking trick that had sort of worked when my cat went missing a year or so earlier. I wrote that he'd be home when I got there, which he wasn't, but he did turn up at 3am that same night. Worth another shot I thought, what else was I going to do as I travelled back from work on what seemed to be the slowest tube in the world.

Will's mum hadn't been well for over a year, having problems with her throat and chest. Although she'd had several hospital visits, she had really played it down. Just over a week ago, she was taken into hospital with breathing difficulties and had since been moved to a hospice, for what we thought was respite.

I'd taken the call from Will about 20 minutes ago and thought it would be the usual conversation about what to make for dinner, or simply checking how my day was going. I couldn't have been more wrong.

"Hello You. You alright?" I said.

"No not really." There was a slight pause. Will sounded

distressed.

"My dad's just called. Mum's developed pneumonia overnight and I need to get to the hospital as she might not last the day."

BOOM! What the hell could I say to that? I was in complete shock. Only yesterday we had spent a good hour and a half chatting to her in the hospital and she was looking better than she had in a long time. Really positive and talking of all the things that needed to be done when she came home.

After I put the phone down I went back to my desk in a complete daze, thinking I can't sit here and do nothing. I had to be at home in case Will needed me. Luckily I was once again working for Henry and we had grown to know each other really well. I approached him as he was chatting to one of my colleagues, but couldn't get the words out. I could feel my lip beginning to quiver. Sensing my distress he ushered me to his office and was very kind and understanding and told me to go home right away. I gave him a weak smile and thanked him before fleeing the office with tears bulging in my eyes and me desperately trying to hold them in. I had an hour journey home via tube, train and car, but it felt like a year.

I kept thinking of happy things or even work, anything to stop me thinking of the situation at hand. I just about made it to my car with a few stifled sniffles and those weird hiccup-like gasps. As I got into my car the seepage had begun and when I got to my front door I leant my head against it as the tears flooded out. I did the first thing that came to mind – I phoned my mum. The realisation that if Eileen didn't make it, Will wouldn't be able to phone her ever again, hit me hard. My poor mother must've wondered what was up when I couldn't speak through the tears. I knew she'd be feeling quite useless as well, because of not living close by. The conversation was stilted but I managed to explain the situation and get out all the disbelief in me, with my mum comforting me.

After I blubbed to Mum, I managed to get a grip for a short time but couldn't sit still, nor watch TV, nor do anything but try not to think about the horrendous news that Will had told me on the phone. He was with his mother now at her bedside along with his father. I couldn't begin to imagine how they were feeling as they sat and watched the life draining from the most important woman in both their lives. Sitting and waiting. I had the inspiration to make some dinner, it felt like a useful thing to do, after all they'd need to eat at some point.

I was interrupted by the phone, it was Will. He sounded much chirpier and told me that his mother was a lot better and that I should come to the hospital. I didn't know what to do. I wanted to be there but at the same time I didn't know if I wanted to see his mother in that state or intrude on this intimate family situation.

The scene that greeted me was one that will stick with me for life. Eileen laid on her back, propped up by several cushions, eyes shut, mouth wide open covered by an oxygen mask. Will and his dad sat either side of the bed holding her hands and they both looked watery eyed but were somehow elated. She was on the mend right?

As we sat and talked I couldn't help but listen to Eileen taking a deep breath in through her oxygen mask and then a painful gap as I waited nervously for the next breath. It always came, but the wait was dangerously long for my liking. My heart would stop in line with her inhalation, thinking that at any minute she would stop breathing altogether.

Will's dad, Geoff, told us to go home and get some dinner and not to worry about coming back tonight as Eileen would likely be asleep. We drove home both relieved, laughing nervously at how upsetting the day had been and how stupid the hospital were for worrying us all; it didn't last long.

Five minutes after we'd arrived back home the phone rang; it was Geoff.

"I just got up to nip home and feed the dog and the doctor said…well..that..although your mum is quieter, she's still not better and that we should stay with her tonight." Will was stunned as he came off the phone, his elation and relief turning once again to disbelief and shock. There it was, everything we'd feared earlier in the day was back like a sharp slap to the face.

I didn't feel it was my place to go to the hospital and that it should just be immediate family. Will reluctantly agreed and went to be with his mum and dad at the hospital.

In some ways I wish I had gone because I was feeling utterly useless at home and couldn't do anything but wait, worry and cry. I found myself in bed talking to a God I didn't believe in, praying that she'd be alright. I had no idea what the time was but I knew I hadn't slept when the phone interrupted my thoughts, it was Will. Eileen passed away just after three in the morning with Will and his dad holding her and trying to calm her as she struggled and fought to her last breath. Will was going to stay with his dad that night.

The next morning he arrived home and I just held him and stroked his hair as he cried his heart out onto to my shoulder. Will is a very strong person and this week was the first time I'd really seen him cry about anything. I, on the other hand, can be in tears watching a soap opera and soon we were both stood there crying as we hugged. We were at a loss for words, yet not really wanting to talk anyway.

He'd just had the worst day of his life. He'd been there to witness the horror of his mother gasping and writhing as the death rattle signalled her final breath. He'd hugged her dead body and sobbed with his dad. It would create a bad last image in his head, but he had to be there at the end, for her sake. He told me he was glad they were there for her at the end so she knew how much she was loved.

Later that day we took Geoff back to the hospital to see Eileen's body. I couldn't stop the tears; it was a truly awful day. That feeling got worse as we went into a side room. There was Eileen except it didn't really look like Eileen, she looked like a rubber puppet. A yellowish tinge, eyes shut and mouth still slightly open. Will and his dad went over to her and held her hand and stroked her face. I stood frozen behind them feeling, once again, like I was intruding on their family's grief. I wanted to run screaming down the corridor but I couldn't. Will turned and buried his head into my shoulder as he silently whimpered. His dad was just staring at the face of his beloved with a little smile of affection on his face as he stroked her hand and the tears gently trickled down his face. Geoff was a proud, old fashioned man and showing his emotions wasn't something he did. He started to talk to her or maybe it was just his inner thoughts. The usual things that you say to comfort yourself when people die - 'She's not in pain any more' was one of the favourite themes. There was definitely a truth to that. She had suffered and her quality of life wasn't great because of her illness. However, I think we'd all still rather have her back, selfish on our parts but we were the ones in pain right now.

I began to question my grief. I liked the woman and in that room I wanted to tell her that I was so grateful at the way she welcomed me into her family, but you wouldn't say we were close. I saw her many weekends and would've done anything for her if she'd asked but really I never saw her unless I was with Will. I was feeling like I had no right to be as upset as I was, but perhaps it was a strong empathy for Will and his dad.

* * *

A week and a half later, and it felt like months had passed. A sombre calm had overcome us all. Life had moved on at a miraculous rate. All that, I suspect, was about to go into reverse as the funeral loomed tomorrow and those horrible memories, tears and questions would flood our minds.

I had several concerns. One being that I wanted to be able to hold Will at the funeral and be strong for him, but most of his wider family didn't know Will was gay, let alone that he had a boyfriend. The second was the anti-climax after the funeral and how Will would cope. He'd have to try and put the grief behind him and move on with his life; a life with a fundamental piece missing.

The grieving process was not one I was that familiar with. The intensity of the emotion in those first few days following his mum's death was so strong that it almost paralysed us and we couldn't get on with day-to-day life. Each day felt like a rollercoaster of emotions where you'd feel ok one minute and the next you'd be crying again.

The day of the funeral arrived and Will and I got dressed in our suits with the customary black tie. I was conscious to let Will have space and take my cues from his mood. He seemed quite together and calm, but I'm not sure how much he was faking it just to get through the day ahead. He looked in the mirror, adjusted his tie knot, gave a little nod to himself and let out a breath,

"Right then. Let's do this."

I squeezed his arm and returned a sympathetic smile as we left the house and headed to his mum and dad's house (I guess just his dad's house now). We arrived to find his dad's cousin and wife laying out trays of sandwiches, sausage rolls and the like (all covered in foil) ready for the wake. We did our bit to help and yet again I felt the great unspoken question – '*Why is this guy here?*' - hanging in the air. To them I was just Will's flatmate. I felt incredibly uncomfortable, but tried my best to be helpful. It felt like months had gone by since Eileen had passed away and keeping busy laying food out, allowed me to keep my emotions in check. Will seemed to be holding up too and was chatting with a few distant relatives who had arrived at the house. A couple of Will's friends had also come to the house first, but I could tell they didn't really know what to say. Will was great at easing their awkwardness and had gone in to full host mode. We were actually having a laugh with Dan and Suzy when, almost as if in slow motion, the hearse drew up with Eileen's coffin visible and a flower garland that read 'Mum'.

I looked at Will and could tell that we were both on the verge of cracking. Suddenly, neither of us could speak. Dan and Suzy, who had their backs to the window, turned to see what we were staring at and instantly their faces dropped too. I managed to signal to Will that we needed to talk in the other room.

Will and I had discussed earlier about what I would do at the funeral with regards to where I sat at the service and which car I'd travel in. Usually, the etiquette is that the family ride in the limousine behind the hearse. Will had said he didn't care what anyone thought, that I was his partner and he wanted me with him in the car. I was to go in the limo with him, his dad and his dads' cousin and wife. He knew I was apprehensive but he had checked with his dad last week and he was fine with it. I, however, still didn't feel comfortable, after all, his mother's funeral was not the place to cause a scene, nor have people gossiping about the strange man stood next to Will. I took him aside in the hall and managing to suppress the urge to cry, told him I'd travel with Dan and Suzy. He seemed relieved. I think his bravado was waning now that he was seeing all his relatives and family friends. He squeezed my arm affectionately and his eyes said it all, he was grateful for me for making the decision for him.

Off I went with Dan and Suzy to the crematorium. I managed to rein in the tears and focus on holding it together for Will's sake. It's silly really, but because I was just a friend of Will in most peoples' eyes, I felt that for me to be crying would look strange. I think, in particular, a grown man crying over the mother of a friend he's only know for a few years is a rare sight. I did what I did at my granny's funeral when I was 12. I played my favourite Kylie songs on repeat in my head and pretended that this wasn't happening. It nearly got too much when Will and his Dad stood next to the coffin to say their final goodbyes before she went behind a curtain and presumably into the incinerator. I could see how upset Will was. I yearned to hold him and reassure him, but I'd just have to wait this one out. I just kept singing louder and louder in my head *'Put your hand on your heart and tell me.'*

That was it. Moments later she was nothing but a pile of ashes that we'd later scatter on a plot outside. As Will and

Geoff stood outside receiving hugs and sympathy from the funeral guests, I joined the queue and waited my turn. I gave Will the biggest manly hug I could and he whispered to me that he was okay. I had an awkward hand shake with Geoff, who gave me an approving nod.

I got a lift back to Geoff's house with Dan and Suzy and made small talk with people, trying to help with ferrying drinks to people as needed. I just wanted to be useful, well actually I wanted to hug Will and collapse on our sofa. The emotional fatigue of the last couple of weeks was beginning to hit hard.

We stayed until the end of the wake at Will's parents' house to help tidy up as one-by-one the guests left and it was just Will's dad, Will, the dog and I. There was lots of silence interspersed with the odd '*Auntie May's looking well*'' or '*Mum would've liked that.*' Time was ticking on and I don't think I was the only one thinking we needed to get home, but I could tell that Will was torn about leaving his dad alone in the house. It was actually his dad who told us we should be going. I think he knew that Will was worrying about him, but he was made of stronger stuff. At least he pretended to be. He's of that generation; '*Death? What you getting so worked up about – it happens to us all, you've got to get on with life.*' That was his attitude and he was right, no matter how harsh it seemed: life is for the living.

The first week after the funeral was the hardest. I'd gone back to work a couple of days after Eileen had died and managed to hold it together when concerned co-workers had offered sympathies. Will was now working for himself and he had to get on and motivate himself. It took a few phone calls but he slowly got back on track.

Chapter 22

As the weeks turned to months there was the happier occasion of my brother's wedding coming up. I was an usher and this time it was Will who would have to fly solo and worry about how to introduce himself to those people who didn't know about us. A fact that wasn't lost on me; I wondered how he'd feel with the shoe on the other foot. To my annoyance however, he didn't seem at all worried, in fact he was winding me up about telling all my aunts and uncles and how he was going to wear a pink suit too.

The day of the wedding arrived, a sunny, bright day in the middle of July and Will was still really relaxed; I was slightly miffed at his calmness, I envied him in fact. I was ok, but not having had any run through I wasn't entirely sure what I was supposed to be doing in my role as an usher.

We drove directly to the church where we met a nervous looking Paul and a very laidback David. The latter making our job as ushers seem pretty straight forward; hand out order of service and say go sit down.

As the guests started to arrive Will made his way inside and David and I began greeting people. I think we did a good job, apart from some old biddie from the bride's side telling us that we should be walking her to her seat, which I reluctantly did.

Will had found some of Paul's friends that he'd met a few times previously and was sat having a laugh with them in the church. After some photos which I decided would be best to leave Will out of (we'd already discussed this – it's my brother's wedding so no shock revelations to my wider family), we went to the hotel for the reception where I was mistaken for the groom by the event planner much to everyone's amusement. I do look like my brother; but not that much.

I caught up with Will as soon as I could and introduced him to a few people. I was feeling rebellious so didn't explain who he was, I just left it to their imagination. I was sure I could hear the light bulbs clicking on with several of my new sister-in-laws friends (*'oh that's the gay brother'* etc). Will seemed to be having a great time. I think it was a good tonic for us both after his mum passing away.

At dinner Paul had sat us with his mates who all knew we were a couple, so there was no awkward coming out to be had. It became a bit of a competition to see who had the most embarrassing story about Paul including a few from the stag do that were supposed to remain secret. This was my chance to tease a few of the guys in front of their other halves. Seeing them sweat as I started to talk about a strip club, then letting them off by saying that we didn't go in of course. The booze was flowing and I was really happy to see Will smiling properly again. I grabbed his arm and pulled him to the dance floor where we got everyone up and doing various dances that are only saved for weddings. We slid to the left, then to right; we pushed pineapples and shook trees; we oopsed upside our heads. We span my nieces around and my mother, as well as any aunties that came near us. Everyone was having such a good time. As the night drew on Will pulled me outside into

197

the grounds of the hotel. He had a naughty smile on his face and who was I to say no?

We made sure no one could see us as we ran off to the gardens and into the maze of fir trees. Will darted off in front of me and disappeared. I ran after him but couldn't see him anywhere. I jumped round the next tree expecting to see him but he wasn't there. My overactive imagination was beginning to move from a rom-com to a horror movie. Was someone or something out here that had gotten Will and was now after me? I crept slowly backwards scanning all round when I was grabbed and thrust against the nearest tree. I was about to shout out but my mouth was sealed with the mouth of another. It was Will and he was kissing me hard. As he let me stop for a breath I told him,

"We shouldn't be doing this." He just laughed.

"I know. Now kiss me."

His hands moved towards my belt and I was completely taken in by the moment. My body tingled at his touch and I knew that I would let him do whatever he wanted and I did. Afterwards we sat smiling looking at the moonlight.

"It's been a great day hasn't it?" I said.

"Yeah, really good fun and I think Paul enjoyed it" said Will.

"What do you think our wedding will be like?" he asked.

"Our wedding eh?" I said. "Is that your way of proposing?" He sat up and looked me straight in the eye.

"You know I love you Gary. Why shouldn't we get married?" I was taken a back.

"Well I suppose there's no reason we shouldn't, but it is really expensive and doesn't really change anything." I said unintentionally putting a downer on the whole thing. Will looked a bit hurt and suggested we go back to the wedding before we were missed. As it turns out we weren't missed but Ian did pick some grass off my bum as we passed him and gave a knowing laugh as I blushed.

* * *

The next day on the journey home we talked more about the prospect of us having a wedding. What sort of a 'do' would it be? Obviously it wouldn't be in a church but neither of us had any issue with that.

"I've always liked the idea of getting married on a beach" I suggested.

"Or maybe a converted barn or country home?" Will countered. We continued to discuss the theoretical wedding and agreed it'd be better than a straight wedding because we weren't bound by tradition in the same way. Sure we could take the best bits from straight weddings, but we could add our own touches. We were pretty sure none of our friends or family had been to a gay wedding before so the rulebook could been thrown out. We agreed we'd have to have a ceremony, but most importantly for us was to have a big party with a playlist of all our favourite songs.

Then came the issues and concerns. Could we stand up in front of our dads and declare our love for each other and even kiss to seal the deal? Would our dads even want to go? It's one thing accepting your son is gay and being nice to his boyfriend, but to see them kissing and being all soppy is quite another. Then there was the question of the wider family especially my aunts and uncles. They still didn't know I was gay let alone considering getting married. Just yesterday I'd had to fob them off with *'Not seeing anyone special at the moment'* when faced with the inevitable '*so are you next then Gary?*'.

Personally, I didn't have a problem not inviting them, I didn't see them that often anyway so would rather pay for my friends to have a nice meal and get drunk with me than my Aunt Georgina. Then again, you had to have family at weddings didn't you?

Then there was the money worry. Weddings are expensive things as my brother had told me countless times in the run up to his. We didn't want to spend £10,000 or more on one day did we? My thoughts were that we should hire a venue and put a couple of grand behind the bar and let everyone get drunk on us and dance the night away. Will laughed at the suggestion but, he could see the benefit. I brought up a final question which lingered between us, '*Who would propose to whom?*'

My main insecurity in our relationship was that I was probably seen as the female of the couple and Will as the male. This was because I had more female friends and he more male. I liked pop music whereas he was more into sport. To all intents and purposes he was more like a straight man and me more like a gay man although I hated the thought of anyone thinking that way about us. Especially his friends. I found it a threat to my masculinity and truth is that we are both equals in our relationship, if anything I'm the more dominant one but I guess that could be seen by some as a nagging wife type role. Will eventually came back with an answer,

"Well it's a leap year next year so if you wait til 29th Feb, you can ask me." Typical that he would make a joke of it. I honestly didn't know whether I would want to propose or be proposed too? The conversation drifted off into silliness as we drove home. The seed of marriage was planted in both our heads, but would either of us act on it?

The answer to that question was to come a few years later when we were on holiday in Thailand in early January 2011. We'd had a great day out on a boat trip, been snorkelling and enjoyed the delicious Thai food. We'd gotten back to our hotel, showered and headed out to the beach for a stroll and ended up sitting on the pure white sands, watching the sun set across the ocean. It must have put us in a pensive mood and we were talking about our relationship and how good we were together. I can't honestly remember which of us brought up marriage, but we'd soon agreed that we should do it.

For the rest of the holiday we proposed to each other a number of times, trying to make use of the many idyllic locations we visited in Thailand. That way, one of them would make a great proposal story. I proposed to Will whilst we sat precariously on top of an elephant. Will proposed to me whilst we swam under a waterfall and so it went on.

When we came back to England we were excited to announce to our friends that we were going to have a civil partnership. We were less excited about telling our parents; it would be like coming out all over again to some extent.

We had decided we'd like to look at venues in Hampshire and headed to my parent's place for the weekend. We hadn't told either of them that we were going to be looking at wedding venues, but then it would be odd if we just disappeared for a morning without telling them where we were going.

I had the coming out nerves all over again and was being abrupt with Will as he tried to give me a pep talk in the bedroom. Although I'd fully intended to come out to my dad face-to-face, I'd failed and Mum had stepped in and done the deed for me. Dad had been nothing but nice to Will and I, but I had the fear big time. As Will was pointing out, we'd been together for over 10 years and had a house together and my mum and dad had been to visit several times. Surely getting married was just another natural step? As much as that sounded rational, I still felt the cramps in my stomach and the urge to flee the house without telling them; running back to my safe bubble.

As we headed into the lounge, Dad was in his usual seat watching the TV and Mum instantly rose to go and make us a cup of tea. When she came back in the room, I felt like it was now or never.

"Mum. Dad. We've got something to tell you." I could feel my dad looking up suspiciously from his newspaper.

"We've decided to get married."

It hung in the air and my dad had a surprised look on his face but didn't say anything. It read as *'What?!'* My mum looked at my dad and nervously got up to give Will and I a hug.

"Congratulations," she said weakly.

My dad's lack of response, I expected, but my mum's reaction was a real shock to me. I thought she'd be over the moon, instead it felt like she was somehow disappointed. I felt the anger build in my stomach, but painted on a fake smile.

"Right we'd better be going as we're going to look at a few venues this morning." Dad was silent and Mum, still a little dumbfounded, managed to wish us well.

Will and I waited until we were in the car and I turned to him and said,

"Well that went well," in my most sarcastic voice. To my surprise he burst out laughing and said,

"I just wish they hadn't made such a fuss." I couldn't help but smile as I felt the anger dissipate and move more to confusion over my mum.

"My dad's reaction, I expected. But my mum – what was that all about?" I said to Will.

"I was surprised by that too. I'm sure it's just shock and she'll soon be offering to help with the food or decorations."

"I hope you're right. She's usually so excited to have a project to get involved with." I replied.

Shortly after, we arrived at the first venue and luckily Will had booked the appointments and had been upfront about it being a civil partnership so they knew to expect two guys. I was relieved that we wouldn't have to come out to complete strangers as we normally would. We were shown around the facilities and then sat down to go through the pricing and options. This was the drill for the next three places we ended up seeing that morning. It was exciting and I'd completely forgotten about my parent's lukewarm response to our announcement until we were parking up once more outside their house several hours later.

As we entered the lounge, Mum had regained her composure and seemed much chirpier and was asking about the venues we'd seen. Dad barely said a word and was very focused on the newspaper. I stubbornly talked loudly to Mum about the venues to make sure he knew this was happening with or without his blessing.

Next day we had another two venues to see and I offered for Mum to come with us. Thankfully, she accepted and we headed off, leaving Dad to watch the Formula One. Once we got in the car, Mum said,

"Sorry to you both if my reaction was a little muted yesterday. It's just that I was more concerned how your dad was taking the news. I think he's struggling with it."

"No shit, Sherlock!" I said sarcastically, before apologising for my language; once a mummy's boy.

"We had a bit of a chat after you'd gone out yesterday and he just doesn't seem to understand why you'd want to get married." My mum went on,

"I tried to explain to him that why shouldn't you, but as silly as it sounds, I think it just reminds him you're…different."

Will could sense I was going to blow so stepped in with a calming word.

"I'm sure he'll be ok with it once it sets in. We've got a couple of nice venues to look around today." That was his way of closing the conversation and I drove on, quietly stewing but knowing he was right to move it on as it wasn't Mum's fault that Dad was being stubborn. She was always playing the peacemaker in our family.

When we walked in to the first venue, both Will and I looked at each other; we were both clearly impressed. Even Mum was getting in on the vibe of the place and was pointing out all the nuances of the décor. I think we knew that this was going to be the venue we'd choose. It was a beautiful 18th century house with a garden that led to a large lake. The big white building was very grandiose from the outside, but it was the high ceilinged entrance room that was causing us all to smile now. Classic, yet simple, it gave off just the right amount of opulence without being too over the top. We were greeted by a very friendly wedding planner called Jean; another tick in the box.

It was obvious that they hadn't done many civil partnerships, but it was clearly an area they wanted to get in to, after all the pink pound was booming. They'd only been legal in the UK for about 6 or so years so the market was still in its infancy. Jean was bending over backwards to point out that we could pretty much do as we pleased with the venue and our ceremony; nothing was too much trouble.

The three of us left the manor house in a much brighter mood than on the car journey and I was relieved to see my mum getting excited and sharing her ideas about table place names and where we could have the photos done etc. It was still in the back of my mind about my dad and his reaction, but that's where I decided to keep it for now. He wasn't going to ruin this experience with his negativity. We were getting married and if he didn't like it, well tough.

The next venue we visited suffered from not being in the same league as the previous one and we barely stayed longer than a quick tour round the building and a cursory chat with the manager.

I asked Mum to give Will and I a minute alone and double checked he was feeling the same as I was about the first venue and he instantly beamed in agreement. As we joined Mum at the car, I told her about our decision and she excitedly hugged us both.

"I loved that one too!" she said excitedly. "An October wedding it is then."

"Yep. Looks that way," I said. "Better get yourself a hat."

We decided that, now we knew the venue, we should check out some of the accommodation nearby to figure out where we would stay the night of the wedding. We had a list from the venue of possible B&Bs and hotels and started with the one within walking distance of the venue.

It was a cute B&B with six rooms set in the Hampshire countryside with a beautiful garden courtyard and fields surrounding it. As the three of us walked in, we were met by a woman in her mid-fifties who had a slight accent that I couldn't initially place. Will explained we were getting married at the nearby manor house in October and asked if we could see the rooms. The woman said congratulations and shook Will's hand and then my mum's hand. Then almost as an afterthought, mine. I thought that was slightly odd, but put it down to the fact that I was standing slightly further away at the time.

She dutifully led us through the corridors and showed us the breakfast room and then a number of the unoccupied bedrooms, finally stopping at the master suite. We are talking about a B&B here so it wasn't luxurious 5 star hotel standard but it was cute and in reality we'd only be flaking out on the bed at the end of a long day of partying. It's location was the main benefit. The owner turned round to Will and said,

"This is where you and your lovely bride would be staying," as she gestured to my mum. I couldn't help it, I burst out laughing. It took Will a second longer for him to click; she thought Will was getting married to my mum!

"Erm..well it's not actually her I'm marrying. It's him." Will said a bit sheepishly.

"Ah. So sorry!." She said and then quickly added, "not that there'd be anything wrong with you two getting married," pointing at my mum.

"Well, I know I'm young looking…" said Mum, trying to get in on the joke.

I think we'd found where we would stay on the night of our wedding. We immediately booked all six rooms knowing that family and friends would want to stay there too.

Once again, when we got back to mum's house, Dad was glued to the TV and didn't even ask how the search had gone. He was making it very clear he didn't want to talk about anything to do with the wedding and this made me both sad and angry. I knew he was never the most emotional of men, but I'm his son and he should take an interest. I was glad to make our excuses and leave Hampshire behind that afternoon.

Will and I were both giddy with excitement about the wedding and the journey home vanished in a blur of who we'd invite, colour schemes, themes, first dances, cake and more. We had given ourselves about seven months to pull the whole thing together.

Most of our friends and family, had never been to a gay wedding before and so we had complete creative scope to be as wacky as we wanted. However, we still wanted people to take it seriously; we didn't want it to seem like a joke.

We ended up settling on a fairly typical set up for the day; ceremony, canapes and drinks, sit down meal and then a disco. We'd allow ourselves the little 'Gary and Will-isms' in our décor and theme and definitely the music.

First though we had to finalise the guest list which was pretty straight forward on the friend front, but not so easy with extended family as many still didn't know I was even gay.

It was time for another potential mass coming out. My biggest problem was with my dad's siblings and in particular a favourite aunty that I hadn't seen since Paul's wedding but who I had many fond childhood memories of. She was very much like my dad, but without a moustache, and she swore like a trooper. As children, my brothers and I loved and feared her in equal measure when we'd go and visit her in the summer holidays. We were still a little scared of her now.

I decided to call Mum and ask her thoughts on inviting Aunty Effoff (Her real name was Ethel but we secretly nicknamed her Effoff due to her potty mouth).

"Funnily enough, your dad brought up that same question

after a few too many whiskies the other night." said Mum.

"Really? I'm surprised he even mentioned the wedding. What was his view on inviting Aunty Effoff?" I replied. I was intrigued to see which way Dad was going to go on the matter.

"He said he didn't think she needed to be invited, nor anyone on his side." she paused.

"I know that's not what you want to hear and actually I will tell you what I told him which is that it's your choice and there's no pressure either way."

After a sleepless night, I arose with my inherited stubborn streak in full effect; I was going to effing invite Aunty Effoff to the effing wedding and eff Dad and what he thought. After all, it wasn't his wedding to control and it's not as if he was interested in anything else about the wedding so far.

I couldn't bring myself to phone her so decided to write her a letter instead. I wasn't quite sure how to start it and after I'd accumulated a pile of scrunched up paper, I decided that Aunty Effoff would appreciate the direct approach. I simply wrote *'I'm not sure if Dad has told you but I'm gay and getting married in October.'* I tried to bury any emotions and fear of rejection I was feeling and continued *'I appreciate that you're from a different generation and so I won't be offended if you don't feel it's something you'd like to attend.'* I included the invite, stuck a stamp on it and headed off to the post box. As I walked, I had a thought that maybe my dad was feeling the pressure of coming out. He wasn't gay, but he was coming out as having a gay son to his family. Maybe he felt the same fear of rejection that I'd felt so many times before? Maybe he was worried that his family would blame him for making me gay or that it would somehow reflect on him?

With these thoughts in my head, my hand hesitated half in and half out of the post box. Then a voice from deep within told me to *'Let go'*. I had to suppress a nervous little giggle, I felt like I'd just done something naughty.

A couple of days later, I knew that Aunty Effoff would have received the letter and anxiously awaited a reply. It came via my mum who phoned me that evening and told me that Aunty Effoff had just rung her. I held my breath as I waited to hear what she had said.

"Well, first of all she said she'd have effing killed you if you hadn't invited her." My mum had what I can only describe as pride in her voice. "She said she will definitely be there."

"Wow…That's great news. So she's ok with it all?" I asked.

"She is. She actually gave your dad a bit of a telling off for not letting her know sooner." I imagined my dad being ear lashed by his sister and couldn't stop beaming. Aunty Effoff had given me her support and hopefully this would make Dad more relaxed knowing that his family were on board with it. I felt a weight lifted off my shoulders.

As the months rolled past and we got busy with the little things like name places and favours, Will and I were thoroughly enjoying the whole process. At times stressful of course, but I think it all added to the upcoming big day.

Then, about six weeks ahead of the wedding, mum rang with some concerning news.

"Look Son, I don't really know how to say this, but I wanted to warn you now so it's not a shock on the day." She said with worry tripping her voice.

"Your Dad is saying that he's not coming to the wedding."

"Oh. Right." was about as much as I could say. Mum tried to tell me how it would still be a great day regardless, but I wasn't really listening.

"Ok. Thanks for letting me know. Bye Mum." I said. As I put the phone down, I was stunned then I quickly became angry as I recited the conversation to Will. What a big man my dad was. He couldn't even tell me himself that he didn't want to come to the wedding. He'd left my poor mother to do the dirty work for him. The irony wasn't lost on me, after all my mum had outed me to my dad, but at least I hadn't asked her to do it. Now my dad was hiding behind her and I was furious. I think I was probably just desperately disappointed. I thought he'd accepted me for who I was and had been nothing but nice to Will. Why would us getting married cause him such an issue? I'm his son and he should just fake it if he had to.

Will tried to calm me down and said that he thought my Dad would still turn up and if he didn't it would be him that's missing out, especially with his sister and other family members going. I thought he might have a point and that Aunty Effoff would no doubt drag him there kicking and screaming if he told her he wasn't going. However, the point was, I wanted him to want to go, not feel obliged to. Both my brothers had gotten married and there was never any doubt that my dad would attend.

I didn't have time to dwell on it as there was still lots to be done. Will and I were doing list upon list of what things still had to be organised. One thing that remained was a reading that one of Will's friends was going to read as part of the ceremony. We'd decided that we were going to write it ourselves and being the more emotional of the two of us, I thought that duty would fall down to me. I was shocked then, when Will sat me down and read me his first draft of the reading. It was beautiful and oozed with his feelings for me. I don't think I'd ever heard him so sentimental. Who knew he had it in him? I added a few bits, including a tongue-in-cheek gay reference just to spice it up and we ended up with:

Sometimes it's the things that come to you late, that are most worth the wait.

A realisation, an acceptance of feelings deep down that can unleash true happiness.

You've taught me what it is to love and be loved.

Always there to lift my spirits with a joke or a smile – you are the magic potion to keep me young.

With you by my side we can achieve anything – a life full of laughter, love, and adventure.

You're a calm port in the storm, the antidote to my chaos, the caution to my gay abandon.

With you I'm at ease, totally yours.

Each day with you surprises and delights, bar none.

Remember always, that with you, I am a better me.

I looked at Will and told him I loved him. I really was lucky to have found someone like him and he'd just managed to surprise me even after all the years we'd been together. I was really looking forward to the wedding, the only cloud hanging over me was that of my dad.

I wondered if I should try to talk to him about it, but we just didn't have that kind of relationship and officially I hadn't been told he wasn't coming; it was only my mum warning me. I decided to ignore it and vowed to really enjoy the wedding with or without him.

As the wedding got closer, my dad's potential absence was looming large in my mind. I'd managed to come to terms with it, but knew it would fundamentally change my relationship with him going forward and make it awkward for my mum in the future. I wouldn't be able to forgive him if he chose not to come to the wedding.

* * *

The night before the wedding arrived and Will and I were breaking with tradition by spending the night together. We'd gone out for a curry with some of our friends and family that had arrived the night before the wedding. We were already feeling the love from everyone and barely slept that night, both being too excited. We were like kids on Christmas Eve.

Morning came and we got ready and both managed to look fairly fresh and very dapper, despite our lack of sleep. I had to fight waves of nerves, joy and anger at my dad as they all took turns in making my stomach churn. I still hadn't heard if Dad was going to be there or not. I was about to find out.

We'd decided to walk down the aisle together, to avoid any 'oh that one is the bride' type comments and I'd asked my nieces to be groom's maids. They led the way and we followed as *Queen* blared out of the speakers; we'd ironically chosen their take on *Here Comes The Bride* from one of our favourite films *Flash Gordon*. I was beaming ear-to-ear as I scanned the room and saw all my friends smiling back at me. Then I looked in the large mirror at the front of the room and saw Dad sat next to Mum. A rush of relief shot through my body; he was there. His expression wasn't exactly one of immense joy, but at least he'd come. I made a point of staring at him and giving him my biggest smile as if hoping it would be infectious.

I didn't have long to worry about him though. By the time we'd reached the front of the room, I turned to Will and he was crying. I hoped it was tears of joy! He looked lovingly at me and laughed as he wiped his watery eyes with his sleeve. A quick glance round the room, told me that he wasn't the only one with tears in his eyes. I could feel my lip start to tremble but fought hard to keep it together – I mean, what would people think if we were both bawling our eyes out?

The ceremony was a bit of a blur. I only like being the centre of attention when I choose to be (usually after a few drinks too) and this was a bit too on show for my liking. On the plus side, everyone in the room was rooting for us and happy to see us finally get married after all our years together. We recited the vows and signed the register, then it was all over and we were sipping Pimms in the garden as Wham!'s I'm Your Man blared from the speakers.

I'd completely forgotten about my Dad, but finally saw him knocking back a beer and chatting to some relatives. He seemed relaxed enough. As the day went on and the booze flowed, he seemed to come into his own and by the time we were sat having our meal, he was the life and soul. He came up to Will and I with a big smile on his face and joked about having chicken at my next wedding. I wanted to scream in his face *'Why did you make such a fuss! Look at you, you're having a great time,'* but it wasn't worth causing a scene. Then I had a serene moment of clarity. Maybe he was just scared of what our wedding would be like and what he might have to watch as part of it. Once he'd seen, and felt all the love our friends had for us and that we didn't have butlers in the buff serving our drinks, maybe he'd realised it was just a great day and got on with it.

After the meal was another moment I'm sure my dad was dreading; the first dance. He wasn't alone; Will and I both had reservations about doing a slow dance. We didn't feel comfortable being so intimate in front of our friends and family who'd probably never seen two guys slow dance. Hell, we'd never seen two guys do it before! Instead, we decided to go the comedy route and had a song with a cheesy dance routine instead; yes the Cha Cha Slide came out early at our wedding. It seemed to go down well with the crowd and soon everyone was up joining us on the dancefloor as the disco carried on through the night.

I felt such acceptance as all these wonderful people were here to support us and give us their stamp of approval. I know that I shouldn't expect anything less from my friends and family, but it was still so uplifting to get validation from them. I took a breather from dancing and went out into the gardens. It was a clear night and the stars shone brightly. I reflected on the last decade and the magic of today and chuckled to myself at how I never imagined I'd be marrying a man. But there it was, Will and I were Mr & Mr and I think I'd finally come to terms with the fact that I was gay.

I was woken from my thoughts by a friend finding me and dragging me back to the dancefloor; Kylie was on!

THE END

Epilogue

There you have it; my coming out story.

I have been really fortunate in the acceptance I've received from friends and family, but perhaps my harshest critic has always been myself.

Reading this book back now, I feel like gay rights and acceptance has come on leaps and bounds since 20 years ago. I also think I've made positive steps forward on my own personal battle with being gay in that time. For example, if I was to meet someone like Carl now, I think I'd find his shtick hilarious and not feel threatened at all. Perhaps that's a confidence that comes with age as much as with accepting my sexuality.

I still believe that who I love or am attracted to shouldn't define me or my lifestyle; everyone is free to be individual. However, I am ashamed at some of the feelings and fears that I've relived in this book, but I needed to be completely honest about that time in my life. It is a journey that we're all on and I'm pleased to say that I'm more comfortable than ever with being gay.

It's rather poetic that as I sit writing this Epilogue, it's actually my ninth wedding anniversary. Releasing this book will be another big step in my self-acceptance.

I hope you've enjoyed reading this book and that if you have been through the coming out process, that you were able to relate to some of my experiences. We are all unique and should embrace that and remember to be kind to others and try to understand our differences as well as similarities.

Acknowledgements

Firstly, I would like to thank the many wonderful people who have put up with me saying *'I'm writing a book'* for the last 15 years. Secondly, to you the reader, my heartfelt thanks for taking the time to read the story of a non-scene nobody. I hope you've enjoyed it.

A massive thank you to Ali for taking my cover vision and making it a reality through her beautiful illustrations.

My sincerest gratitude to the many people who have read the book (in its many drafts) for all their wonderful feedback. A special thanks, in particular to fellow author Clare Lydon for all her help and guidance. If you love reading romantic fiction, please do check out her body of work.

Finally, my heart belongs to the real life Will for giving me the best years of my life. Long may it continue. Love you!

CONNECT WITH ME

I'd love to hear your thoughts on my book and would be very grateful if you could leave a review on Amazon plus you can connect with me on Twitter or drop me an email as follows:

E: GaryHJames@virginmedia.com

T: Twitter.com/GJ_EntFocus

Printed in Great Britain
by Amazon